FIFTY YEARS
WITH
HARNESS HORSES

CLAIR WOLVERTON

FIFTY YEARS
WITH
HARNESS HORSES

By
CLAIR CUTLER WOLVERTON

THE STACKPOLE COMPANY
HARRISBURG, PENNSYLVANIA

Printed and bound in the United States of America
by THE TELEGRAPH PRESS, *Established 1831*
Harrisburg, Pennsylvania

TO MY WIFE

OLIVE

for her inspiration and understanding

FOREWORD

Ofttimes the quality measure of a product is not deter-
mined by the fame of the producer. More than rarely the
writer of commanding lines has given no predecessor bearing on immortality. Yet how often do we find productions
well worth while, where the keynote is conveyed through
some factor quite foreign to the present product.

This scribe is not here attempting to convey the accom-
panying effort to literary heights. Instead, after a pleas-
urable perusal, he classes it as the sincere appraisal of an
honest and interesting writer, whose story compasses near
to a life extent. That this life activity was greatly occupied
with the training and racing of trotters and pacers does
not indicate that the writer was devoid of the necessary
sense of literary building. Rather, in this humble estimate,
there is the impression that the gift of fair self-expression
was here turned to one whose life work carried into a
foreign field.

Inevitably, too, personality must enter. Over a rather
extended period, this writer has known Clair Wolverton,
and without detracting a bit from his racing and training
accomplishments, it may be said that one of his most commanding features was a sterling honesty that prevailed
under all circumstances, including some that must, at least,
have been trying. It is true that such an endowment does
not insure literary achievement, yet in the nature of man-
kind, the inclusion of such pronounced probity is notable.

The training and driving profession is one that bears many irksome factors. Jealousies and bitter contentions are often at hand. Yet, over many years of acquaintance with Mr. Wolverton the writer has yet to hear from him any word of detraction of a fellow reinsman, or fellow horseman, of any branch. A kindly, quiet, restrained personality blotted out grossness and unkindness.

Necessarily, his production brings in numerous reflections upon his training and racing activities. Here, too, it is easy to sense the unselfishness and modesty which so definitely prevail in his life story. Brothers of the sulky profession are given a sincere measurement through the Wolverton standard; self-appraisal, particularly self-glorification, are not evidenced.

Possibly the factor of personal friendship may influence these words, though in all truth, the effort of this scribe is definitely towards an honest portrayal of this reinsman-writer. Honest fellow men are not exactly rare, but those who carry the scale-balancing to so delicate a conclusion are not too many.

It appears that numerous horsemen—many through personal acquaintance—will take enjoyment in this plain relation of equine lore, including absorbing facts about great horses and horsemen. And the writer of these lines will be exceedingly glad if through some clumsy phrase of his added attention may be turned to a production both interesting and sincere, written by one who has given freely and well in this thing we call life.

GEORGE M. GAHAGAN.

CONTENTS

Chapter I

EARLY MEMORIES

AFTER sixty-seven years I am taking a pleasant memory journey back over life, re-appreciating the legion of blessings which have been mine. I have lived to see that some of the things I thought I wanted and which were denied me, would not have been nearly so good for me as those I actually received. Also I have lived to see that the added crosses of our best standard breeds have evolved a very distinctive type. They now look like trotters and pacers.

Going back to the Big Creek Stock Farm owned by my father where I was born May 16, 1886, my first memory was of brood mares and little colts that were hoped to be future greats; and what breeder does not have that dream even though unexpressed?

The farm was located about three and one-half miles east of Chalmers, Indiana, on land that would compare very favorably with any in the state. About twenty acres in one corner where the house and barn were located was thickly studded with walnut trees. The framework of the training barn, which was a hundred feet long, was comprised of walnut hewn and morticed beams.

My father had a pretty good black-soil training track, and I remember in particular a three-day race meeting he gave. An owner-driver had a little gray pacing gelding

1

The training stable and the stallions on the farm of the author's father.

hitched to a high-wheel sulky with pneumatic attachments, which, incidentally, was the first kind of sulky I can remember. On this occasion the cinch broke, letting the shafts fly up, and the man lit sitting down in almost the identical position he had had in the sulky. Luckily he was unhurt, and to my boyish eyes it looked very funny.

That was about 1895, not later than 1896. My father had about forty mares and their foals for at least past two-year-olds. To me, a little boy, they represented the very best in the trotting world. However, added years and experience tell me that perhaps three or four mares had any license to produce speed. A mare called Lizzie R. by Cutler, 2:24¼ pacing, produced several standard performers. In fact, all that we produced that amounted to anything were her foals. Her dam was by Robert Bonner, a son of Hambletonian 10. Although my father never broke Lizzie R., I can remember that she was a keen-looking little mare. He used to remark what a good-gaited trotter she was in the field. I recall that he bought two mares, one Margaret by Onward, 2:25¼, and the other Favor by Sidney, 2:19¼, grandsire of Lou Dillon, 1:58½. They were nice mares in those days.

How well I remember our stallions! Crayon portraits of them hung in our living-room. One was Dick Red, 2:34¼, trotting register 10849. He developed leg trouble, otherwise he would have gained a faster record even in those days. They all said he was a good-gaited trotter. Crossed on to mares sired by Cutler, son of Strathmore, 408, he produced most of the performers Father had.

Then there was Byerly Boy, 2:30, by Byerly's Abdallah, dam Lucy Gurnett by Warwick Boy, Byerly Boy's register number was 10848. (I am quoting these register numbers from memory. I could be wrong, but I don't think I am.) Byerly Boy, as I remember him, was a nice brown horse.

Not much of a sire, he got his best record rather late in life after making several stud seasons. He was a little foul-gaited, too. I often wonder if he might not have been a pretty fair trotter with our present-day training methods and shoeing. They always talked about how game he was.

Cutler, 2:24¼, pacing register 4665, was another of our stallions. He had been accidentally blinded in one eye. A nicely made little horse, he might have trotted with our present-day training. In those days time was suppressed. He undoubtedly could have paced much faster than he did.

I remember that he was a terrific puller on the race track. In scoring for a race at Wapakoneta, Ohio, he fell, throwing his driver, Fred Glazier, who went as high as the lines with his hands through the holders would let him go. He went on over, lighting on his back, and remained unconscious for thirty-six hours. My father, who remained with him, often used to talk about it. At the time Fred was quite young. Such an accident probably would have killed an older man.

My father bred and raced runners before he got trotters. He often used to laugh about the trimming he got with them. He retained a throughbred stallion called Young Albion by Oltawa, known around the farm as Little Dick. This was a beautiful chestnut and raced good. He was a fine road horse and the people from around the county considered themselves lucky to have a road horse sired by him.

Even as a very small boy, how I loved and admired the horses! A little foal with its mother was about the most wonderful thing in the world to me. I remember my father taking a yearling filly (later named East Lynne) and another brown filly which afterwards produced John S., 2:10, and several other record foals to Delphi, Indiana, to be broken and trained. The trainer there was Dick Berry, who really had a lot of ability and who later moved to Indianapolis, where he developed many horses, one of which was the mare Argetta, 2:08½, for the M. L. Hare Stock Farm. Art Alco, 2:08¼, and The Bishop, 2:09¾, and The Hero were also among horses he trained. Subsequently he ran a public stable until his death when he was fairly young.

In partnership with Berry in Delphi was A. A. Jackson, who came the next spring to our farm. He had read the novel *East Lynne,* and among the horses he developed were colts named from characters in that book, such as Kennelworth, East Lynne, West Lynne, Arthur Carlyle, Dick Hare, etc. East Lynne later got a record of 2:14 and was the fastest performer bred at Big Creek Stock Farm. She was a beautiful mare and was my property for a time after her racing days were over.

Being a believer in heredity and its effects on the horses, I, boylike, began to wonder why I was so intensely interested in the horses and what inherited influences made me tick. I learned that my grandfather, Philip Wolverton, (Mrs. Wolverton tells me that the name Philip means "a lover of horses") accumulated some 2,000 acres of land. Each of his children by a former marriage was given a hundred-and-sixty-acre farm. Busy though he was, he kept a few quarter horses around, and Father used to tell me he had known him to bet as much as five hundred dollars on their chances. That was when money was money. Also he laughingly told me about him and his father slipping his own and his brother George's ponies out at night and giving them a trial and then approaching George for a bet.

My father, Philip Wolverton, was to my mind a wonderful judge, especially of type, of a trotting stallion. He used

to point out to me, a little boy, the good and bad qualities
of the cuts of stallions on the front page of *The Western
Horseman.* All through the years I have purposely drawn
out horsemen, especially those I considered good judges
of type, etc. I have yet to find one who seemed to have
anything my father apparently did not know.

He truly loved horses, and to this day I have never seen
anybody with more ability or better judgment in breaking
a colt to drive. He had unusual hands. I have seen many
a colt going along cheerfully with its ears set forward,
wearing a double wire bit. He had a system that I am
not sure would not be good today. We had a road cart
with a pole in it, and a pony, a clever, smart little horse
that knew all the angles. We generally would drive the
colt several days on the near and off side, after which we
would hitch it single. Very few ever gave any trouble and
soon were driving nicely.

When I grew large enough to help, my father made me
very proud. I overheard him tellling somebody that he
would rather have me than a big older man on the guy
rope because I seemed to know when to pull and also
when to release it quickly.

To my knowledge he never drove more than two or three
races, winning two of them. He did not seem to care
for it. As the memories come I recall what a kidder he
was. The times I was the object of his banter may have
been, I flatter myself, because I could take it so well. To
this day I can hardly resist the temptation to tease people
I like. I remember how people loved to loaf around my
father's barn and how they would follow him around at
our fair after we moved to Lafayette, Indiana, and accept
his advice about what to bet on in the little book that was
set up in the center field. It used to amuse me as a small boy
to hear him talk, at the same time using a little mannerism

all his very own, telling people he thought the last colt, meaning, of course, Lizzie R.'s, was the best colt the old mare ever had. I used to chaff him about it. As I write this I can think of two more fillies out of Lizzie R. that would surely have reached had they been trained.

Proudly he used to tell me of Mother, a teacher of a near-by country school. She died when I was about three years old. He said they had not been married six months until she knew more about the blood lines of the trotters than he did. Like most women of that era she could drive a road horse, as that was the necessary method of transportation. In her case she was very expert. She used to drive, so a groceryman from Monticello once told me, the stallion Cutler, 2:24¼, and also the thoroughbred stallion Little Dick. He said she would have us little children with her, load the buggy with groceries, and drive back home, a distance of nine miles. As I have mentioned, Cutler was a terrible puller on the race track, yet my father declared he drove gently for her on the road.

My Grandfather Cutler on my mother's side used to castrate our colts every spring. He was a good judge of a horse himself.

On the other hand, when my Grandmother Cutler came to visit us, I always hid all my horse papers. Knowing that she was a staunch Methodist, I thought it diplomatic to tell her that when I grew up I might be a Methodist minister. I doubt now if she was much impressed. She had been a country school teacher and the mother of five children, and probably knew I was trying to put a fast one over and thought it wise to let me think I was.

I have three sisters, Margaret, Pearl, and Ethel, and they all like horses. Don't tell me there is nothing in heredity!

Again, our own children, Philip, Selma, Ken, and

The first horse of the author. The pony at the left.

George, all have an unusual liking for the horses. Any one of the boys can get into a sulky and rate a horse almost to perfection. In these days they are busy with their professions and seldom ride after the horses. One season we took George out of college because we thought he was studying too hard. He helped me work the horses and would cut the pace out while I trailed him. I never saw him fail to get us over to the half more than a half second out of the way. I used to be amazed at my son's natural skill. Some of their ability they no doubt inherited from their own mother, for since they are grown and in their own homes, Mrs. Wolverton travels with me a great deal. She has observed much about the horses and is getting so she can spot lameness very quickly. Too, it has pleased me greatly because she has made many friendships with other horsemen and their families.

But to go back to my childhood. The first horse I ever owned was a pony we called Texas. How I loved him! He was a little gray gelding, sired by a Shetland stallion, and his dam was a gray Indian pony mare. My father raised him for me, and when the pony was about eighteen months old, broke him and got a cart so that my sister and I could drive him to our country school a mile and a quarter away. Father constructed a little shed on the school grounds in which to keep him during the day. I was then about eight and my sister younger. When school was out in the afternoon the pony was good and ready for his trip home, and brother, *we traveled!* After we moved to Lafayette that smart little pony became our road horse, and the whole town grew to know him. Two of my sisters and another little girl all used to mount him at once and ride up a steep little hill there in the fair grounds and purposely fall off of him. He would wait patiently for them to remount. He used to be able to unhook or unlatch his stall door and get out unless it was very tightly fastened. Once outside, there was a hydrant near that was easy for him to turn on with his nose and get a fresh drink. It was a good thing he could not talk or he would have made a touch on me sure. After Father died and he was about sixteen, I pensioned him on my uncle's farm where he spent his last years in a good big pasture with other horses for company.

While the horses were my paramount interest, it must not be presumed that I spent all of my time at the stable, the pasture, or the track as a small boy. Like other children, my sister Pearl and I had our childish diversions. I chuckle as I remember one occasion when we were throwing pebbles at a brood of baby chickens a short distance away, which certainly we were not supposed to do. Pearl knocked one over and, perceiving that I had not seen the accident, she said: "Come on, I'll race you to the barn." Of course, once at the barn I was interested in the horses and, while thus absorbed, Pearl slipped back and hid the dead chick in the weeds. Soon we were both back again throwing stones at the chicks and this time I killed one. I turned to Pearl for counsel. We decided to bury the chick in the garden. Now that I also was guilty my canny sister stepped over to some weeds and showed me the chick she had killed. Guilty consciences made us confess to our auntie, who was housekeeper, and we were forgiven.

Probably for sheer grace of movement no other animal so nearly approaches that of a race horse as does a deer. Thinking they would be of interest to visitors to our farm, Father purchased from a friend in Monticello a few deer which had been tamed. He decided to build a small pen and put the little fawns in it, so that they could be handled. While he was building the enclosure he turned one of the does and her fawn into our dooryard, which was rather large with some tall grass in it. To me little fawns are beautiful with their rows of white spots in their coats. They were beautiful and intriguing to me then, a small boy. On this particular day I had gotten to within a few feet of the fawn when its mother gave a signal by stamping the ground with one foot. The fawn dropped instantly into the tall grass where it was hard to see. I took another step nearer and glanced around just in time to see the doe standing on her hind legs and coming at me with those sharp cloven hooves. She only struck once, as I was already on my way in the opposite direction and no doubt lowered any record they have for that kind of running.

In the spring of the year when the old buck is shedding a furry substance from his horns, he is cross. I remember one morning when my father took feed into the pen, the old buck charged him and brought him up over a high fence that ordinarily it would have taken him a long while to climb. At that he was gored badly enough that he was in bed several days.

To me, a little boy, those deer were wonderful, and I still like to think about them today.

The panic of 1895 practically broke my father, making him lose his fine farm. In the fall of 1897 and the spring of 1898 he moved our family to Lafayette. He and another trainer and a groceryman became partners in the training of horses. Also, they held a speed sale at the fair grounds. These birds really trimmed my father in one season. The following season he opened a colt-breaking and training stable. I got my start as a trainer there at the early age of fifteen years. My first race mare was a nice free-legged very muscular mare, Ella Red, 2:12¼. How I loved her! For years I found myself comparing other horses I trained to her.

In 1898 at our fair in Lafayette, I had my first look at a

Left to right: Ella Red and Lucy Wilkes.

great horse, to be followed down the years by a legion of most of the great harness horses. Dan Patch, 1:55¼, which had made his first start at Boswell, Indiana, where he won with ease, was stabled in the barn we called our training barn. Accompanied by my father, I was a visitor to his stall, where I hung on every word of his friendly care-taker. I believe that even the people realized he was a great horse. Like most of us engaged in the horse business, I had my pet superstitions. To avoid any kidding I might get, I generally slipped the horse or colt that I liked best in our stable into the stall that had been occupied by Dan Patch. I never said anything and I doubt if anyone ever suspected my real reason for placing them there. Among the horses that were placed in that stall was Ella Red, 2:12¼. She was a beautiful pacer. Another was the yearling colt, Turk McGlory, that afterwards got a trotting record of 2:13¼. I did not give him his record, but he was the first of quite a lot of good yearlings that I trained. I was quite a proud boy-trainer because Turk McGlory trotted for me in an eighth in 20½ seconds timed by Sterling R. Holt, who happened to be a visitor at the Fourth of July meeting. Mr. Holt owned Maywood Stock Farm, the home of Rex Americus, 2:11¼, this colt's sire, and he also owned Sidney Dillon, sire of Lou Dillon, 1:58¼.

However, to continue with Dan Patch. Come race day and Mr. John Wattles, his driver and in all likelihood the real reason why Dan happened in the first place, was in the sulky. He probably had more ability than anybody at that time in that section of the country. To me he looked a proud old gentleman wearing chin whiskers. A pretty good-sized field started. He elected to start his drive shortly before reaching the three-quarters. This equine express looked to be simply flying. He appeared for all the world like a big schoolboy pushing a lot of little boys out of the way on a playground. The judges announced he had paced the last quarter in 30¼ seconds. My sharp eyes had seen him throw a hind shoe. It had sailed away up high much as one would sail a pie plate. He lost the heat to a horse called Milo S. by a head, one of the only two heats he ever lost. He won the succeeding heats easily. His owner, Mr. Dan Messner, was surrounded by his friends and fellow townsmen in the grandstand. I was a short distance away and eagerly drank in all the good-natured wisecracks. What a day for a horse-loving boy!

Dan started twice more that fall and ended up with a record of 2:16 made at Brazil, Indiana. He was then shipped to Terre Haute in the same state. He did not get to start there, but his owner finally contacted M. E. McHenry. He had written him much earlier in the season. It seems the letter would get to each town just after he had left. McHenry got Dan later in the winter and raced him down the Raging Grand, losing the only other heat Dan ever lost to May Marshall in 2:08¼. He was shipped home that fall by express and the little town of Oxford celebrated his home-coming in gala fashion. Nothing like it had ever happened before. His record time was 2:04½. Dan was shipped back again to McHenry. Later he was sold to M. E. Sturgis of New York City, who later sold him to M. W. Savage of Minneapolis, Minnesota; and it is reported that he made a fortune for this last owner in being used to go exhibition miles and for his advertising of International Stock Food. Nearly every schoolboy and girl in this wonderful country spoke of Dan Patch just as in later years children would speak of Babe Ruth. I have heard that Mr. Savage was very fond of Dan Patch. At any rate it is said that he died only three days after Dan. In after years I used to listen to men I admired get to bragging about the chances they had had to buy Dan Patch. I would have believed them about anything else, but I just could not help but laugh a little to myself about that.

While Dan got the world's record of 1:55¼ pacing behind a training cart drawn by a runner and with a canvas between the wheels and also another runner at his side, the powers-that-be decided not to recognize any more records made that way. While Billy Direct and Adios Harry since lowered it in the accepted way to 1:55, I still wonder sometimes if this freak horse with his wonderful mental equipment and a gait different from that of any horse observed before or since, really tried as hard as the champions that followed. All any of us can do is guess about Indiana's amazing horse.

Joe Patchen, 2:01¼, was one of my idols when I first became horse conscious. He was reputed to be a very beautiful horse and was the sire of Dan Patch. He had a mannerism which Dan Patch also frequently exhibited, that of turning his head and gazing into the grandstand when coming back from a false score. He raced against Star Pointer, Robert J., and Frank Agan, 2:03½. Joe Patchen often beat Star Pointer although the latter was the first horse to pace in two minutes.

I personally believe that Dan Patch was probably potentially the fastest horse that ever lived.

While on the subject of Dan Patch I must tell this. William Fry had established a new sales barn down on the levee in Lafayette, and a few years after Dan's appearance he had gotten consigned to his speed sale Kingston Patchen, a full brother of Dan. Mr. Wattles had passed on and Kingston did not have the advantage of his advice and training. He came to the sales barn about two weeks ahead of time. As I used to lead with a pony and also drive the horses that did not have somebody with them to show them, the first morning I had them run a pony beside him while I drove him. This appealed to his sportsmanship, and how he would race that pony! Accidentally I had stumbled on to the answer. After we had shown him on sale day the boy said to me, "Clair, this is the only horse that can make this pony straighten his neck." I had instructed my good friend, P. J. Kennedy, to bid my all which was about $800. After this was passed he stepped over to the cart and said: "Clair, I am going on and I will stand in with you." He took him on and when $1600 was passed he decided he was the victim of by-bidders and stopped. And he was. Kingston was taken back to his owner and sub- jected to the same methods. But he developed trouble in a suspensory ligament and never raced. What a keen looking, nice horse he was! Fate and its vagaries had kept me from a chance to drive what would probably have been a great horse and a first.

The spring I was fourteen years old my father had traded me the mare East Lynne, 2:14, for a colt he had previously given me. She had a colt about a week old by her side. Father and I boarded up her and the foal in one end of a box car with plenty of straw. I got into the car to accompany them to Washington, Illinois, to the farm of A. G. Danforth & Son to be bred to the stallion Sphinx, 2:20½, by Electioneer, to which I had booked her. When we got to a division point I had become too cold for comfort and crawled over into the straw with the mare and colt. I fell asleep and finally awakened to find the little colt's mane brushing me in the face. How it could lie down that close to me with its little back to me and not awaken me, I will never know. Anyway I was comfortable and I have often thought how cute it was.

In 1901 I began my career professionally. I, being a mere boy, of course did about everything but drive a race. I was only fifteen years old and not nearly so rugged as any one of my sons. I would have been scared to death for them to try it, although they would all have liked to have been drivers. As I think back, I realize what a good fellow my own daddy was with patience galore! After my first race, which was plenty bad as the mare was badly outclassed, he comforted me with: "Clair, maybe she will do better next week." And indeed Ella Red was a lot better the next week and from then on.

CHAPTER II

EARLY YEARS OF RACING

THE next year, 1902, I invaded the Great Western Circuit with Ella Red. It was then I met some of the truly great drivers of that day. Among them was Al Thomas, who was in charge of the stock farm which, at that time, owned the stallion The Conqueror. He also had a horse called The Merchant that had taken a yearling record of 2:29¼. Even then he was an aged trotter, but he was a good-gaited little horse and got a record of 2:13¼. Mr. Thomas was accounted the most expert of all time at leading colts with a pony. He used to show the colts at Madison Square Garden. He was a man with a lot of ability and was an outstanding horseman in his time.

His son Henry, who is one of our great drivers today, was a youngster then, and gave what was probably his first trotter a record that week at Joliet, Illinois. Around the barn the colt was called Rags. Young as I was I could see that Henry was plenty boy for anybody to rear and it was a good thing he had Al to do the job. Since then he has driven a lot of great horses and done a great many things with horses.

Al Thomas in his own right was a very rugged man. It is said he used to drive a stage coach in his early days. In his prime he was considered one of the most versatile and virile of men. He had tremendous vitality. He used to show horses at Madison Square Garden, then known as the Old Glory Sale. In 1910 on my way to Nova Scotia I stopped off at Madison Square Garden where he was leading colts. I remember one instance. Blue Feather was a colt in the Walnut Hall consignment. He had shown him and the top price offered was around $300 or $400. Mr. Thomas asked permission to show the colt again and gave him such a showing that he sold for around $3,200.

In later years he gave the trotting horse Mainsheet a record of 2:05. I overheard him say that that summer the horse ran a temperature every week and this he kept down by administering a drug, the name of which I do not remember. Mainsheet sired Mainleaf.

Al's second son, Arthur Caton Thomas, was once engaged in the newspaper business. Walter Palmer, called the poet laureate of the horse world, wrote a poem entitled, "With the Trotter in the Stall," which was quite popular. Arthur wrote a parody, which was one of the wittiest things I have ever read. One line was: "How do you find his velvet nose when he has distemper?" I had a copy of this parody once, but unfortunately I lent it, and like so many things that are loaned it was lost. I deeply regret that I cannot reproduce this poem in its entirety.

The same season brought me a glimpse of Oscar Ames, who had the brilliant trotter Angiola, 2:06. And I met George Loomis, who was a truly great horseman. The work he did with Sir Roch, Hollyrood Walter, and Pearl Benboe, 2:02¾, was really outstanding. He did not believe very much in disclosing to anyone the workings of his mind. In later years I grew to know him and his witty wife and enjoyed them immensely.

Then there was Dick McMahon, who could drive as good or better when a great deal of money was being bet.

In fact, he bet a lot of money himself and always carried large sums on his person. It was pretty well known among horsemen that he could and would fight and they never worried about his being held up and robbed. I saw him often in the years that followed. He could do things.

Also among those drivers was Charley Dean. His work with The Broncho, 2:00¾, and later with Minor Heir was remarkable. He had many other good horses. He was a lovable fellow, but like Dick McMahon he also would fight. In those days it was not unusual for drivers to exchange blows. They would do things to each other in a race and afterwards fight it out.

There was some I do not recall, but I do remember Bert Higbee, McLaughlin, and Charley DeRyder.

Many of these drivers, whom I met for the first time back in 1902 when I began to race in the Great Western Circuit, have passed on, but I feel sure that those skillful, alert, quick-witted men with their natural horsemanship, if suddenly transported into this era, would acquit themselves very creditably alongside the trainers and drivers of today. Nor do I want to detract anything from these fine able men of the present. However, I do believe the horses of those bygone years required more skill to rig and balance them than in most cases do horses now. Remember, the horses of today have many more inherited crosses of established gait to draw from.

This brings me to another observation. Recently I found a horse paper which revealed that John R. Gentry, 2:00½, had been timed an eighth in 12½ seconds. In Mr. Geers' book, Robert J., 2:01¼, is reported to have had terrific brush. Elastic Pointer, 2:06½, is said to have paced an eighth in 12½ seconds. Joe Patchen, that made a sensational campaign, is reputed to have had extreme brush. Lafe Schaeffer told me that Mr. Geers once worked Walter

Peter Manning 1:56¾ with the beloved "Pop" Geers up,

Direct, 2:05¾, a quarter which he would never reveal, but which was a real hair-raiser. Thus progress in breeding has not increased speed much, but the added crosses in intelligent breeding have produced a lot more horses which can go very fast. This skillful breeding and growing has done much to increase, too, the number of extremely fast two- and three-year-olds. Also the shortened style of racing plus the many more places to race have helped.

In this memorable year of 1902 I was to see the man race who was not only the ideal of my boyhood but of my manhood as well—Mr. Geers. What George Washington was to America and the American army, what Abraham Lincoln was to his country and the saving of it, Mr. Geers was to the harness-horse world. I believe that he was the most outstanding horseman, not only of his time, but of all time.

Our 1902 racing season ended, as usual, with our fair at Lafayette, which was the last few days of August and the first few days of September. The Grand Circuit meeting at Terre Haute was to follow, and I decided to see my first Grand Circuit racing. Therefore, in company with Al Drum, our trusted caretaker and friend, who at that time I believed knew all about everything, he being much older than I, we hied ourselves to The Hut (our name for Terre Haute). It would naturally be supposed that I was anxious to see the racing, but my secret reason was to see what Mr. Geers looked like and how he drove.

That season, as I remembered it, he had in his stable The Abbott, 2:03¼, the then world's champion trotter. He also carried Direct Hal and several other exceptionally good horses. I saw him drive the horse Prince of Orange in a race there.

Incidentally, this was my first glimpse of Ben White, who was Mr. Geer's second trainer and who is, to my mind,

Rosalind 1:56¾ with the veteran Ben White in the sulky.

one of the truly great trainers today. At that time he was a very young man. I find myself wondering why it is that he has had so many frictionless-gaited trotters through the years.

But going back to Mr. Geers: I have had the privilege of seeing him drive many outstanding races. Among them I particularly remember the one at Lexington with William O., where, in my honest opinion, it was his driving and not the tired pacer which was responsible for the victory.

Another great race he drove was with My Rosebud at North Randall. I feel sure she was not the best horse. The way he drove Napoleon Direct, 1:59¾, and won at Lexington, wherein he was reputed to have paced the last eighth in 11¾ seconds after having made a break and caught—I could go on naming many races he drove but these, to my mind, of the ones I saw, were the most remarkable.

In later years I used to spend much of my time loafing around the Geers stable. Louis Arnold, who had worked for my father when I was a small boy, was one of Mr. Geers' grooms. I liked Louie and the acquaintanceship gave me a good excuse to be at the stable in my spare time. A few years after that, imagine my surprise when, one afternoon at Cranwood Park, Ohio, Mr. Geers, who was sitting behind me in the grandstand, stooped over and invited me to ride with him to the hotel in Cleveland. I was greatly flattered and let him do nearly all the talking, although I was fairly bursting with things I wanted to discuss with him. He was often referred to as "the silent man from Tennessee," which naturally made me more quiet. He took me by the old Glenville track, which is now converted into a residential section.

Years later he and I, at his suggestion, made a few small bets on horses. I forget now, but I suspect we made a little

Snap Shot, 2:08¼, champion four-year-old gelding of 1904 and the author's first fast horse.

money. I would have bet on any horse he named just because it was he who named it.

I always enjoyed talking about him to Lafe Schaeffer, one of his second trainers, and to Mr. Kopf, his blacksmith for many years. The number of incidents they related would make a book.

A number of years ago, in conversation with George Foster, who at one time or another had been employed under Mr. Geers as second trainer, he told me he had had a letter from his wife. In it she said that she had taken their little boy and called on Mr. Geers at the Buffalo Grand Circuit Meeting. He took the little fellow in his arms and the tears streamed down his face. She knew he was thinking of his only son, Walter, who was killed while·in college by a pitched ball in a ball game. It is said that he was so grief-stricken that he sat all day facing the wall and not speaking.

It was after this son that the horse, Walter Direct, was named. He was one of his favorite horses and could probably brush faster than any horse he ever drove. He was undoubtedly much faster than his record indicated. He was later lamed in his stall due to the fact that a laundryman drove his horse close to the outside of the stall and excited Walter Direct.

Mr. Geers' death at Wheeling, West Virginia, behind a trotting mare which had caught her rubber boot and fallen, killing him at the age of seventy-two years, always saddens me. He was not only my ideal, but beloved by every horseman who knew him.

As I think of it now, no driver had his horses' attention as he did. It seemed to me they were intent on his every signal and command, paying no attention to other horses or things. I always thought a horse would make more of a supreme effort for him. The horses, Saint Frisco

Miss Leo Rex, 2:15½, a sister to Tiverton, 2:04½.

and Anvil, would very likely not have been such great horses in other hands. And there were doubtless many others that I can't think of or don't know about.

The year 1903 found me still racing Ella Red and one or two others of quite a little less ability. She wound up the season with a record of 2:19¼. It must be remembered that horses were then classified by record instead of money won. It was quite possible for a horse starting in a slow class to win a heat in 2:10 or 2:12, get distanced the next heat and in a week or so find himself starting in a fast class without having won any money. It became a habit of those selecting entries for their fairs, etc., to ask you what record your horse had and promise to keep him in that class even though you went much faster.

I remember a case in point several years later. I started a three-year-old pacing filly for a friend of mine. She actually paced in 2:17¼, finishing well back. The winner paced in 2:11¾, but the time was announced 2:29¼ in order to keep him in the 2:30 class. It would be very hard to convince me now that our present mode of classification is not much better for everyone concerned.

In 1904 I began to get results. That year, in addition to Ella Red, I had the four-year-old Snap Shot, 2:08¼. He was the champion four-year-old gelding of the year and tied the four-year-old record for the year. He was high-keyed and really a good pacer. He had gotten a record of 2:21¼ the season before when he was three.

This was to be my last season with my first love, Ella Red, 2:12¼. I had given her her record, winning a seven-heat race at Chilicothe, Ohio. As I remember it now, I never had a horse come from behind her at the head of the stretch and beat her. True, she had been beaten many times, but they had always had her beaten before we got to the stretch. We sold her in the Indianapolis sale that fall.

I was now anxious to try my hand on a trotter, so we bought, in partnership with a local lawyer, the mare Miss Leo Rex, 2:15¼, full sister to Tiverton, 2:04½. My eagerness got me outsmarted as the man who owned her knew that she was thirteen years old that spring. She had been through a lot. I was careful all winter with her and although she had been a terrible puller, the next spring I could work her in 2:50 and shake the whip over her back. It was extremely hard to find races for her, but finally I won one or two.

A funny incident happened at New Albany, Indiana, where they had an old mile track. As I recall, it was about the last fair held there. There could be only four starters and our mare was among them. One of them was a gelding with a record of 2:18¼, driven and in charge of one of those old fellows who had the race won beforehand. He had promised to let one win the first heat to get a record so he could be retired to the stud as he was very unsound. The other horse was to be glad to go along for the ride, as they used to say, and the little he could win. Boylike, I could quickly see that he did not know about our mare and did not even consider her. After sizing him up I went to Mr. Ed Murphy, the groom, and told him to say as little as possible about our mare.

On race day I noticed the old fellow only jogged a couple of miles and turned ready to race, something I had never seen before and have never seen since. I decided I could outtrot him unless he was different from any driver I had ever observed. I kept the mare in behind him in the first heat to the head of the stretch. He had set an easy pace to that point and I brought the mare out and she fairly flew by the surprised man. He came to our stall after the heat with good, friendly advice to the boy driver. The next heat I could see he was going with me and we trotted to the quarter in 32½ seconds where he made a break. The race was easy from there on. I had lots of fun about him, for he had planned to get the best of that green boy and old man. I always thought by the way he drove that first heat he was a very surprised man.

I have mentioned Mr. Ed Murphy and I want to add that he was the most skillful feeder of a harness horse I have ever known. He was a natural horseman and I learned a great deal from him. He was one of the best judges of conformation I have ever met. Most of his life was spent with runners. I confess I teased him, but he did have a great deal of influence with me when it came to horses.

The following season I went to the races with two of the worst knee bangers that I have ever come in contact with in my whole life or even seen. They had been in the hands of Billy Marvin. I raced one of them, a free-legged, steady-going stud. One could have tabulated his pedigree on the back of a postage stamp and still have had room for his name and address. One day he came clear around behind where a knee boot fits and cut gashes where the knee folds, with enough blood running down to drown a mouse. He stood between heats undistressed and appeared in no pain whatever. I put a pair of Bystander knee spreaders on him. They were—at least the ones I used on him—made of hickory slats attached at the shaft and extending above the shoulders with the tops connected with elastic. They reached from the shafts down to a point about even with the knees and were elastic from there to the foot. It seemed to me that usually elastic would break at a critical moment. And one day an elastic did break just as a pacer was coming up, the stick came out between his legs and nearly tripped him. A cartoon of that pacer and me in a Ft. Wayne, Indiana, paper made me laugh and see the ridiculous side of it.

Ed Murphy, one of the finest grooms of his time, holding Toma Hanlon.

I started one day in Illinois and was second to the half in what I thought was pretty easy going. I decided I would wait until I headed down the back stretch before I began my drive. I finished a bad last and had to draw him before the next heat to keep him from being distanced. He had gone his all before he had reached the half and I had been certain he was going easy.

The other pacer was a son of Dan Patch, dam by Venture, 2:09½, a son of Bald Hornet, a great old Indiana sire. He was meant for a very fast horse if he had not hit his knees so hard. Our track at Lafayette was pretty dusty. One day in training he went into the first turn so fast I could feel the sulky slipping. I gave him a breeder's record around 2:12 at, I think, Decatur, Illinois. I raced him at Quincy, Illinois. We had a pair of inflated knee boots on him. Going away the first heat he tore the boot in two, a piece of it flying with the speed of a baseball by my head. I fancied I could see his knee swelling on the way to the stables. We put spagnum, which is a moss used by florists, on his knee. What a mess! I came home chagrined and decided to be more discriminating but still keep trying. I have always observed that nearly all horses that hit their knees are meant for fast horses. Some veterinary who understands it some day will fire along the weak cord and help some of them.

The next year, among others, I trained Royal Lancer, 2:15¼, which was one of the two colts my father bred from the two mares he bred to Rex Americus, 2:11½. My, but he was a fast three-year-old pacer! He paced several eighths in 14½ seconds, which is still pretty fast for brush over a half-mile track. He won four of his six races and I sold him to Mitchell and Adams of Halifax, Nova Scotia, for whom in 1910 I went to Halifax to train.

In 1907, two years after the death of my father, a lot of

Royal Lancer, 2:15¼, held by Ed Murphy.

my pet theories were knocked into a cocked hat. A farm boy came in with a pacer he used on the road, and un-hitched him from a road wagon. The horse paced an eighth in 16½ seconds. The Crouches, famous as importers of coach and draft horses, immediately bought him for $400. They had a trainer and kept a few of the harness kind. They did not discover until too late that the pacer had been overheated. A smart guy from downtown sold the farm boy a chestnut filly for that $400. This filly, then a three-year-old, I had broken and put to pacing and she had been turned out. We all thought she had been sold plenty good at that time. She was sired by General Smith, 2:20, a beautiful horse in the show ring, winning many blue ribbons. His breeder's record had been given him, so I am told, by a shyster trainer who had waited until nearly dark, run him most of the mile except where the judges could see. He had sired Captain Crouch, 2:11½, considered a fair pacer for those times, Prosperity Bill, 2:12½, a really nice trotter, this mare, and a few others. I would not have considered breeding to him for a first-class horse.

This filly's dam was the most beautifully colored chest-nut I have ever seen and was a nice mare with speed on the road. I don't remember the little breeding she had. This young man, the son of a responsible, well-to-do farmer, took the filly home. He was too lazy and trifling to feed and water her properly. He made arrangements with me to train her the next spring. She came to me thin and weak, but trained much like any other green filly until I got to going in 2:20. Then I discovered I might have a real green pacer. I started her around July Fourth in a slow pace. She was not only steady, but could have won easily every race in which she started. As I have said, in those days if you won a heat you might get a record that might put you in a faster class. Then if you were unlucky you might get distanced later in the race, get the record and no money. About a week before the fair at Ft. Wayne, which had a mile track, some of my friends who were to race against me said, "Clair, if you race that mare against us any more we will make a kick, and you will have to win and get a record on her." I was afraid to start her at Ft. Wayne, but I worked her in 2:09½. I went back and brushed her in 29½ seconds.

I started once more against Red Bow in a fast class and was an easy second. Red Bow, 2:04, had just come from Lexington. Albert Merrill of Danvers, Massachusetts, had started the filly I was training in one of her races in Indiana. He sent Charley Doble out to buy her for one of his patrons. Charley, who was a really nice fellow also, was the brother of the famous Bud Doble, whom I had never seen. It was early·winter. We finally closed the deal on Sunday. I called the owner and told him I would bring the money —about $2,000—on an early morning train. He told me his wife had said, "My, aren't you afraid Clair will keep right on going to Chicago with all that money?" An interesting thing about the mare was that she required an unusually wide sulky. Horsemen of that day thought pacers that went wide behind could not be good horses.

What happened to the farm-boy owner of the filly? Well, an old cheater in a near-by town thought he would like a big chunk of that money. He went out to his local track and moved the eighth pole. He then had the farmer time him a fast eighth. Then he sold the worthless trotter to him for $1,600 or $1,700. I did not train this one, but I heard he was not registered with the American Trotting Association, but with some wildcat association of which I had never heard. The horse, of course, did not make good. I did not see the young fellow for two or three years. When I did see him he told me he had gone from bad to worse and his wife had left him; that he had been in Chicago for a while and gone good and broke, but that one day he decided on reform. He rode a freight train to Lafayette and walked several miles to his father's farm. His father, in addition to farming a lot of land, had a contract to gravel a road. At the time he related all this to me, he was running a five-hundred-acre farm belonging to his father, had it well stocked, and his wife had returned to him. From a lazy, worthless beginning he had become a hard worker and a good manager. I was still a young man, but it knocked all my preconceived notions a twister because I remembered he had once been too lazy to walk out to the track to see his own filly work. Maybe you, dear reader, can figure it out.

I had been breaking to drive a big percentage of the colts in the vicinity of Lafayette for several years. In 1909 I purchased the horse Spooney Boy, after seeing him second to Gypsy Woodland in 2:07½. This was the first time I remember seeing Everett Osborn, who drove her. He was a very young man then and is among our top responsible reinsmen of today. This was Spooney Boy's first race of the season and he was starting very much out of his class. He could not have won if he had tried. The horse was entered and paid up in a few one-thousand-dollar stakes. I went to Logansport, Indiana, and found the owner very discouraged. He was sitting on a trunk, waiting to ship him home, after having raced him out of the money in his first stake. I bought him for $500. He was a poor feeder and his groom, in an aside, told me to feed him and keep away from him as much as possible. This was supposed to be the best way to handle him. I soon found out that the opposite treatment was the best as he seemed to crave the companionship of his handlers. I loosened his hopples four holes and won two of his remaining stakes and placed second in his last one. One

Miss Harris M., 1:58¼, driven by the "Wizard of the Reins," Thomas W. Murphy.

of these was from a field of seventeen horses at Frankfort, Indiana. I was a little proud of this race. I gave him a record of 2:10½. I sold him just before I went to Halifax for $1,000. It seemed to me then that I had a lot of money. He was a slick-gaited pacer, a good-headed horse, but rather frail.

Late in January, I, who had never been farther from Indiana than Ohio and Illinois, made my first big trip. I went to Halifax, Nova Scotia. I was a pretty green young man and probably looked the part. I stopped off in New York a day or two to attend the Old Glory Speed Sale.

In Halifax I trained the Mitchell and Adams horses. I found our neighbor horsemen a delightful lot and very capable. There I met Frank Boutellier, trainer of the Edwards Stable. Also there was Frank Powers, the starter, who was a pretty good one, too. Then there was Peter Carroll, who later trained and raced the trotter Bill Sharen. As some will remember, he was a stake trotter for the great driver, Thomas W. Murphy. I thought Peter Carroll really had skill driving a horse. In later years after I was back in the States, I knew Peter's son Jimmy, who was a very nice fellow. While in Halifax I met George Leavitt from the States. He was a supersalesman and some high class horses passed through his hands, among them the stallion Todd and, I rather think, his sire Bingen, 2:06¼. He was up there selling a Gambetta Wilkes mare to one of Boutellier's patrons. I had the impression that he really knew his way around. There were many other nice fellows there whose names I cannot now recall.

As I look back I think that of them all, Mr. Adams was the best judge of a harness horse's capabilities. His son Frank, slightly older than I, was another whom I admired and liked. He later owned the stallion Watchim, which, I am told, is a really good trotter. As I have said, I had sold

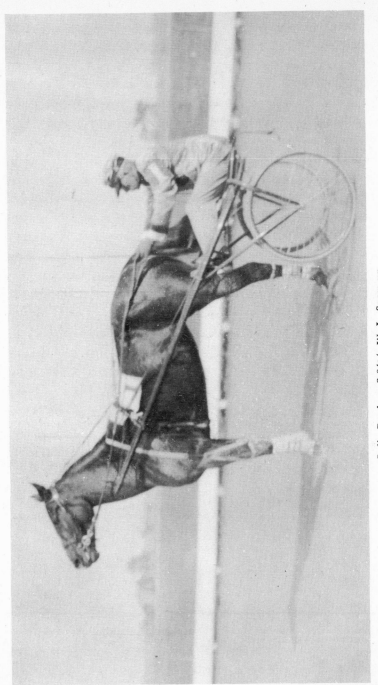

Lelia Patchen, 2:04¼, W. L. Snow up.

Royal Lancer to the Adams and Mitchell Stable. That was the way I had made their acquaintance. That year this stable was the largest money-winning one of the Maritime Provinces. For some reason at that time American horses were barred and we only had about forty horses to compete. Frank Patch was undefeated and Alice A. was the champion mare of the season. Frank Patch ended the season with a record of 2:14½. He was sent to the States the next year and got a record of 2:05½ in the Walter Cox Stable.

Mr. Adams used to tell me the air in that country slowed the horses about three seconds. Royal Lancer, the horse which got me the job, raced disappointingly, although he had worked in 2:10½ and a quarter in 29½ seconds before going to Nova Scotia.

I prevailed upon Mr. Adams to let Frank drive Frank Patch in his last race at Halifax. He won easily and Frank got a lot of pleasure out of winning in front of home folks. I was always glad I did.

That was the year of the Jeffries-Johnson prize fight. I bet twenty-five dollars with one of my owners on Johnson because I thought he would win and he did. I am not sure it is good judgment to bet with one's owners. A near riot broke out the next day at the track between the whites and the blacks. One little old policeman prevented it. I was on the spot where I would have been right in the middle of it, and was I scared!

That fall I returned to Indiana with a very high regard for Nova Scotians, and thought I was a very traveled young man.

The next year I trained again at Lafayette. Among the horses was a mare by Klatawah, 2:05½, the then champion three-year-old pacer, her dam by Dan Patch. She was a free-legged mare and rather peculiar. I beat a pretty good pacer with her one day. She got a half-mile track record of 2:11½.

The following year, 1912, I trained again at Lafayette and raced in Michigan with fair success. I came home to a mare I had left behind for more training. She was Leila Patchen, 2:04½, a record she got later. She was a free-legged mare until she had raced quite a lot. I raced her very carefully the next year, keeping her eligible for the Chamber of Commerce Stake, for 2:23 pacers. She was a good mare and I sold her that winter through James Clark for the account of Aaron Williams. I did not meet Mr. Williams for a year or two. He was a high-class gentleman, whom I admired greatly. He later became prominent as one of Walter Cox's owners. We all think of Walter as one of our very foremost trainers and race drivers. At the time Mr. Williams owned Leila Patchen, William Snow was training some of his horses. Mr. Snow was among the top trainers of that day. Toward the close of his career I got to know him and once had a very pleasant ride with him from Lexington to Cincinnati. I could see he knew his way around.

Let me add that the Chamber of Commerce Stake mentioned above was very attractive to owners and they would pay a good price for a horse eligible for that race if it looked as if he would have a chance.

As I remember, the following year on P. T. Strieder's advice, I trained in Ft. Wayne, Indiana. Nothing outstanding happened in the horse department, but I did meet a number of fine fellows. Mr. Strieder, of late years, was connected with one of the big Florida fairs.

The following year I returned to the Lafayette track. Among the horses was Laddie, purchased by Mr. Marvin for the account of A. E. VanNatta, who had just owned William, 1:58½. Marvin had bought Laddie from Jad

Steadman, who first trained Independence Boy. This horse later got a record around 2:01½ and was a great horse for Charles Valentine. Valentine not only became a very colorful figure through the years, but a very successful one, too. Laddie did not ready very early when Marvin shipped him away and he was shipped back to me. Later he did get ready and pulled me a quarter to a training cart over our old home track in 29½ seconds. He was a fast horse, but was not game enough, but even at that he raced pretty good for me.

Those years I was around the great William Marvin a lot. In that part of Indiana we, at least, considered him the best race driver in the state. He was really good, and to this day I think he could hang a set of hopples on a horse better than anybody. I remember seeing him stand up to a horse in the cross ties, holding his hands out about even with his legs, then go back into his office and come out with a set of hopples that the groom would not have to change that season. Successful as he was with the hoppled kind, his greatest horse was a free-legged pacer, William, 1:58½, considered one of Indiana's foremost horses. He was training one day at Columbus, Ohio. I timed the first eighth away from the wire in 13¼ seconds. William was broken and received his first training as a two-year-old by George Welsheimer, a pretty bright fellow in his own right. He worked him a half in 1:05 to a much heavier training cart than is now in use.

Just before our fair at Lafayette, he had worked this half over a track that was never considered very fast and was a little long. Immediately all of us were sure he was going to be an outstanding horse.

The next season he was turned over to Billy, as we called Mr. Marvin, and here he came. Just before time to ship away, Billy worked him in 2:13½. I was jogging a horse

at the time. While William was being taken to the stable,
Billy waited to tell me how fast he had worked him. The
average young horse that could go from fifteen to seventeen
would generally get so he would win a few races that
trained here. Well, we all went over to Terre Haute with
blood in our eyes for his first race. As I remember it, Single
G. and a good three-year-old called Little Bernice were
also making their first start. William beat them and made
them like it. Mr. VanNatta, his owner, dear old P. J. Kennedy, George Welsheimer, and a few others and I went
over to bet on him. I think P. J. bet on him pretty heavily
for those times.

That fall William lowered the world's record of 2:05½,
held by Klatawah for several years, to 2:05 at a race in
Springfield, Illinois, I think. He looked fairly easy to me.
He was certainly a good fast horse. Marvin once told me
that if they had kept on racing Directum I. against him in
those match races they were having that Directum I. would
have gotten so he could not go in 2:15. Directum I. later
held the world's record without a wind shield of 1:56¾,
until lowered by Billy Direct to 1:55.

Just think, at that race in Terre Haute Single G.,
William, and Little Bernice, none of which wore hopples
and all destined to become great horses, were making their
first start!

The year 1916 found me again training at Lafayette.
Among the horses was a mare the name of which I have
forgotten. She was a fair green pacer and probably would
have raced creditably had she had a few more races, but
she went lame and I did not get to race her much. Her
owner was a Mr. Johnston, who lived on a farm near Otter-
bein, Indiana. He had taken his loss like a good sportsman
as all good owners do. We were very good friends, but I

did not see him again for several years. One day at our fair in Indianapolis he came, bringing me as a present the set of harness he had bought for that mare years before. I had been away from Lafayette so long I had almost forgotten him. He said he was too old to farm and at his closing-out sale he had reserved the harness for me. I was deeply touched, and it renewed my old belief that there is a world of goodness, kindness, and generosity in everybody if we but look for it.

The year that I trained Mr. Johnston's mare, I gave yearling training to some colts that later became pretty fair trotters. Among them was Checkers, 2:06½, owned jointly by my good friend John P. Foresman and myself. He raced remarkably well for the Allen Brothers and for others, too. Two others, Peter Lafayette, 2:06½, and Lady Wilgo, 2:05½, got their last racing with Lon McDonald, one of our great trainers of that time. The one that I thought was really better than they was Pearl Axworthy, 2:19¼, with which I won four of her six starts over our little old half-mile track. I found she could brush very fast and would not break. I used to take them away very fast and, while they were recovering from their breaks, I would get a chance to rest her. While she really trotted in 2:16¼ when she got her record, a veterinarian told me she had a cyst up in her head which interfered with her breathing. I find myself wondering if she could have had a trip to one of the real top veterinarian hospitals and had had a high-powered veterinarian remove that cyst, maybe I would have had a trotter of the Grand Circuit variety. It is something to think about anyway as she had everything else.

While on the subject of Pearl Axworthy, I feel I must give credit for much of her success to a caretaker I had. For Pearl Axworthy not only had the cyst which I have mentioned, but she was almost blind. Even though he was a terrible drunkard, this caretaker was always gentle and kind to her, and would lead her around very carefully because of her faulty eyesight.

The next year I went to work as a trainer for the Crouch Stock Farm, shipping the above-mentioned colts, along with several others, over to the Indianapolis State Fair Grounds. Indianapolis has been my home ever since.

Just before shipping we traded for Hegler, sired by Hedgewood Boy, 2:01, his dam Etha R., 2:12½, trotting. Since his sire, Hedgewood Boy, was a pacer, after breaking Hegler, I naturally tried to train him on the pace; but that gait was not his preference, so we trained him on the trot. He could trot pretty good that fall, but the next year, as it looked as if I would have to join the service in World War I, the contract with the Crouches was terminated and Hegler was turned over to Mr. Geers that fall. He wintered him at Memphis and what a trotter he looked to be the next racing season, working in 2:07 before he started!

That spring of 1917 I was to see my first and only Kentucky Derby. In company with Clarence E. Cole, I met on the train going to Louisville the great Knap McCarthy, a contemporary of Geers, McHenry, Alta McDonald, Jack Curry, Lon McDonald, and all the rest of the great drivers of that time. It seems he had abandoned the trotters for a period and trained runners instead. Being with him was like wearing a special badge, as everybody seemed to know him. I remember that in the morning I was in the stall with Omar Khayyam, which was the winner that afternoon. I noticed that among other feeds he had a plentiful supply of mixed hay, at least half of it clover. In those days we horsemen believed that a harness horse should have only straight timothy hay during training, that mixed hay was not so good for their wind, etc. Many of our horses would not eat much hay especially in hot weather. After seeing

Omar Khayyam that afternoon I made up my mind to try mixed hay on our trotters, and I have been very well satisfied with the results. That fall or the next Mr. McCarthy was at the fair ground and remembered me. I was quite flattered as he was a really great trainer. Over the years myriad are the stories told about him and frequent the quotations. He was one of those fellows who believed in himself and well he might at that. He was killed in a racing accident that fall.

Clarence Cole had shod the fair grounds horses ever since I have been located in Indianapolis and I think several years prior to that. It was at the suggestion of Alonzo McDonald that he located there. Before that he had made regular trips down the Raging Grand where, at one time or another, he shod all of the great horses of that period. There is no doubt he is at the top of his profession. Each year at our state fair the Grand Circuit horses and their trainers flock to his shop. Probably no one knows more of the important trainers and owners than he. Sometimes, when he was not busy and was in a reminiscent mood, I have had a lot of pleasure listening to him tell of the horses and the doings and sayings of great owners and trainers of former years.

CHAPTER III

EARLY YEARS WITH LA PALOMA

THE YEAR 1918 was the most important of my life. Lady Luck was racing in my colors and on May 16th, which was my birthday, the lovely Miss Wolever joined me in marriage. The ceremony was performed by her minister cousin, and after he had pronounced the marriage benediction we were away to a flying start. Careful always to observe its solemn promises, we are reaping the beautiful rewards we hoped for. We have four fine children who have adopted integrity as the keystone of their lives and thereby brought us much happiness.

The Crouches had purchased the great William at the Old Glory Sale after he had proved a great disappointment to C. K. G. Billings, who had even turned him out for a time on one of his farms. The Crouches put him back in Mr. Marvin's hands, but he was never again to reach the high form he had been in before. That fall, at our fair, William had won a rather close heat from Miss Harris M. Mrs. Wolverton and I were in the Crouches' box when that grand old gentleman remarked, "I wish it would rain." "Why, Pa, why do you want it to rain?" demanded his wife. Clearing his throat, he replied, "Because we need it." I could tell that Mrs. Crouch did not get his drift, but I have had many a good laugh over it since. There was only one J. Crouch. Miss Harris M. won the other two heats.

La Paloma, 2:01¾, with the author up.

After the races that fall I decided I had better go into the service of our country, so I took a job in a defense factory and worked there until the armistice was signed. The next season I raced a few horses here in Indiana, among them the aforementioned Pearl Axworthy.

The next year, 1920, I raced a few horses and won a race over Hegler with a mare who could trot in about fifteen. She could not trot nearly so fast as Hegler, but this poor horse was now trading-stock and was simply out-lucked by the mare due to his failing eyesight. Because of his eyes he had a broken neck a few weeks later in a racing accident. Some day I hope racing officials will bar horses with defective eyesight. I have raced two or three with faulty eyesight. One of them was blind in one eye, yet he was the champion two-year-old pacing gelding of that year. However, I still believe it is not only dangerous but wrong to make such horses compete with those with good eyes.

Things were really beginning to happen to the Wolvertons now. One day in early December while I was home at noon I said, "Abiram Boyd is advertising a weanling filly by Walter Direct, 2:05¾, in the *Western Horseman*. Wish someone would buy her for me. I look for him to be a great sire some day." Part of my thinking had come from James Hazelton, who had Walter Direct in charge. Jim, to my mind, was a great stallioneer. He was not only a good judge of horses, but he seemed to have an uncanny knowledge of why some horses should be outstanding sires. He once told me he had trained the stallion Anderson Wilkes, 2:22½, and had driven him a mile in 2:16. He said he was not only a nice horse but a good trotter. He not only sired the wonder horse Single G., but a lot of other remarkable horses. Effie Powers, 2:08½, took many a first-rate free-for-all pacer into camp for the half-mile tracks.

At this time Walter Direct was just getting nicely started as a sire.

Mrs. Wolverton answered me with, "Why don't you ask Mr. Fox? He is a great friend of the Crouches."

That evening I went over to his house and after we had talked a while he promised to meet me at the Union Station and go with me down to Cambridge City to see her and buy her if we liked her.

Before Mr. Fox became wealthy from oil wells, he had run a string of oil-well tools, and in some kind of an accident with them he had lost a leg. Only a few years after the incident concerning the filly he promoted the first Fox Stakes, today the most important stakes for two-year-old pacers.

The night before our proposed trip to Cambridge City it turned very cold. The next morning I was at the station as agreed and he came stalking in. "Clair," he said, "all the water pipes out at the farm are frozen. You go on down there and if you like the filly, tell him I will send him a check for her."

Mr. Boyd had brought his colts in to an old unused livery stable in town and had Howard Vickery breaking them. Howard was the first man who raced the great Single G.

As I strode into the driveway there was Howard hitching the filly. Before I came within fifty feet of the bright-eyed, unusually muscled little filly I had made up my mind she would be a member of the Wolverton Stable. Although not over nine months old, she was pretty well broken to drive by the time she reached my stable.

Before I was married I had often amused myself by going out to the parks of the different towns and cities in which I raced. I could not dance, but I liked to watch others do it. At Decatur, Illinois, the band played a tune that made quite an impression on me. I did not know its name until the next year when I was riding from Lafayette, where I was training, to Indianapolis with the VanNattas. One of them was Earl VanNatta, who owned William. The conversation turned to music and I told them about the piece I had heard at Decatur. Jack said it was called "La Paloma," which is the Mexican National air and means "the dove." I was as charmed with the name as I had been with the music and mentally decided to give a horse that name if I ever had the opportunity.

A few days after the filly had joined my stable I told Mr. Fox I would like to name her. With a remark typical of him he said: "Go ahead. I don't care what you name her."

And that was the entree of the great mare that put the Wolvertons on the map. Now she has passed on, but her family still carries on. Her daughter, Her Ladyship, 1:56¾, world's champion pacing mare, was also a phenomenal brood mare. The combined sale of Her Ladyship's produce has reached enormous figures up to now.

Among La Paloma's progeny were Carty Nagle, 2:00, and Anton Lang, 2:00½, both real horses. Still Waters, 2:05½, produced several good colts and had she had the same chance earlier in her brood-mare life as Her Ladyship, perhaps she might have been a great brood mare in her own right.

At different times I have wintered weanlings and as I kept them in the training barn, I would generally break them to drive. On nice days during that winter I would jog La Paloma a little. In May I trained her some, never going more than an eighth of a mile with her. She paced an easy eighth in 21 seconds, after which I sent her to a farm and had her given grain twice a day. After the races in the fall I had her brought in and I jogged her all that winter. While

she was trained around 2:17 or 2:18 as a two-year-old,
nothing extreme was asked of her. As yet there was no in-
dication of her being the fast mare she proved to be. Just
now I can't remember the other horses I trained and raced
that year.

The next year when she was three, I trained her around
seventeen quite a little. One day I said to my second trainer,
"This filly should now be ready to work in 2:15." Suiting
the action to the word I stepped her over to the half in
1:07¼. She surprised me by pacing in 2:12¾ handily,
coming the last quarter in 30¾ seconds, fairly flying the
final eighth. I had a real pacer from then on. In that mile
she threw a curb and was a little lame on it for about three
weeks. She was shipped to Muncie, Indiana, for her first
start, a three-year-old pace. She raced about three-eighths
of a mile and from then on to the end of her career she
seemed to know every angle of racing. As I remember it,
she was an easy second to Charles Boswell driving a good
filly, sold later for a long price to the great Thomas W.
Murphy, our leading driver at that time. That particular
filly was owned on that occasion by Thomas Stahl of Padu-
cah, Kentucky, whose horses seemed to beat me as many
times as I beat him. He always seemed lucky and every time
I raced against one of his horses it was he I had to beat. I
have had some good laughs when he has been in an entertaining mood.

I shipped La Paloma to New Castle, Indiana, the next
week. She was still a little lame and I approached Charley
Boswell with the proposition to split first and second money
and go an easy pace. He looked at me, grinned and said,
"Well, you know Mr. Stahl." I replied that I did. I went
easy with La Paloma and had to be content with second
money, since I could not bluff that old boy. I next shipped
her to Frankfort, Indiana, the following week. By now she

was sound, so I started her in a slow class for older horses. She was again an easy second. By this time I was beginning to bow my neck a little, for I could see she was going to be a high-class mare.

The next week I shipped her to Milwaukee to tackle the real colts. Dick McMahon had a good three-year-old filly, the name of which I don't now remember. It being a state fair and no betting, he bet a couple of hundred with Johnny Austin on his filly. I don't think he knew anything about La Paloma and did not even consider her. I brought her out from behind him at the head of the stretch and won. When we pulled up he said angrily: "Now you have done a smart thing. You have marked your filly." As I have previously mentioned, in those days horses were classified by their records and not by their money earnings as they are now. I did not answer him as there was nothing to say.

I could not go to Springfield, Illinois, so I had my friend Billy Marvin drive her and she won handily. The following week at Indianapolis I drove her. A few weeks earlier I had said to Mrs. Wolverton, "I wish La Paloma could win at Indianapolis and the band would play 'La Paloma.'" I had forgotten about making the remark. In the race she was following the lead horse and could not get out until nearing the seven-eighths pole when the lead horse accidentally bore out and she went through like a baseball thrown to win. She won the other heat easily. And the band did play "La Paloma" while I happily followed her to the stable. Her last race of the season was at Converse, Indiana, where she was again an easy winner.

Success with La Paloma began to attract a number of Walter Directs to my stable in the next few years. I remember that at one time there were eight of them. One thing I found in common with all of them: they would do about everything you wished they wouldn't do. They would hang

La Paloma with the author up winning at Columbus, Ohio.

in their training several seconds from where you thought they ought to be going until you were about ready to give them up for a bad job. Then some morning you would awaken to find their bad habits had disappeared and they could go the distance—go fast and race good. I really liked them. One of them, a horse called Prince Direct, I raced through the Grand Circuit about as I raced La Paloma. I remember at Lexington I either gave him a breeder's record of 2:04 or worked him that fast. He was a fast, game, free-legged pacer. Before I got to race him the next season he hurt himself in his first start, breaking a bone in his hip. Another driver was handling him.

A year later I raced him and won a race with him over a half-mile track. Two others out of that bunch raced well for me—Elizabeth and Martha Direct. They both produced record performers. Mr. Haskett owned Martha and he and I remained warm friends until his death.

We decided to race La Paloma down the Grand Circuit the next year at four years and not give her a win race record, thus keeping her eligible for the stakes and at the same time decide if she had class enough for the job. I timed her in one of her races in 2:02¼ and allowed her to win a heat one day in 2:05 and a fraction. We brought her home that fall feeling we were able to tackle big game the following year.

The next spring I was working horses one day and did not notice that one of the fair ground wagons had crossed over to the center field way up the stretch behind me. When I came around where the wheel tracks were, the mare jumped them and fell, throwing me out. I got a slight concussion, which kept me in bed a couple of days. It was about time to tighten up La Paloma for her first start at Cleveland. I had William Cooper, who was helping me train, come over to the house, and we decided to work her

Anton Lang, 2:00½, winning at Lexington, Ky.

around 2:10. I had always trained her and she knew me. She was a wise little old owl and when Bill got her around to the three-quarter pole he saw she was not going fast enough and struck her a sharp blow with the whip. I will always think the surprised mare kicked before she thought. Up until that time anybody could work her. My brother-in-law liked to work horses and I used to let him give her some of her letting-down work in the fall. Well, she had learned to kick and let me say she got to be one of the most expert I have ever seen. She could hit the cross bar of a sulky and barely tighten the kick strap. I have broken many colts and thought I knew a lot about kickers, but she was in a class by herself. She had as much skill kicking as a good prize fighter has with an upper cut.

My experience has been never to hit a horse that is kicking or trying to kick, but to divert them, if possible, and rig them to prevent as much damage as possible.

By being careful she had not kicked all the latter part of the season. She paced a fair race at Cleveland and a better one the next week at Kalamazoo. The following week at Toledo I timed her in 2:02 to be second or third. From then on she got good and was always in there pitching.

At Kalamazoo I had been in the Walter Cox Stable and a friendly groom had told me they were carrying along a horse called Northern Direct on which they intended to bet some day. I had forgotten about it, and when we raced at Cleveland in a class race I figured La Paloma should win handily. Just before the race somebody came over to me and said, "The betting looks a little funny, Clair, over there. Are you trying?" I told him that of course I was. I took La Paloma to the front going away, something I did not generally do, especially if I thought she was in pretty tough. Going down the back stretch I noticed that Cox was trailing me with Northern Direct and then I remembered what I had heard. Going around the upper turn I tried to start her up to keep him from catching me with a rush at the head of the stretch. My signals to her, however, were of no avail. Although she was wearing a blind bridle, she was going with him step for step when he pulled out on her at the head of the stretch. That last quarter was a sizzler and she won it by a head and a neck. I had timed the mile, but not having a split second watch, I could not time the last quarter. I went down where Walter was and he told me the last quarter was in 28 seconds. She won the other heats quite a little easier. Never a brilliant training mare, yet on race day she was a "natural." She was dead game and had what horsemen call class. Her colts seemed much like her.

She won several races that summer. Among them was one at Milwaukee which prompted Mr. Trussler of Madison, Wisconsin, to buy Anton Lang from me at weaning time. It was in the contract that he was not to change the name I had given him. Bible readers will remember that Anton Lang was the real name of the person who took the part of Christ in the Passion Play, which was enacted in Oberammergau every ten years. Aside from its significance it is a beautiful sounding name. Anton Lang, the horse, had such a good foot they would remove his shoes every race day. Mr. Trussler told me very recently that he believed that had the pace been cut out faster in the earlier part of the mile that he would have paced even faster than the 2:00½ he paced at Lexington's Golden Strip. If readers look it up, they will find he won a lot of races during his career.

That summer we raced for the biggest purse for which I had ever raced—$25,000 at Kalamazoo. Come race day the starter finally told us to mount our sulkies and score our horses down a time or two before preparing for the start.

La Paloma was going bouncing along, threatening to kick. Big Dick McMahon had a roan horse, the name of which I do not now remember. Anyhow he was coming down very fast directly behind me. La Paloma, being a small mare only fourteen hands, two-and-three-quarters inches tall, he almost ran over me before he saw me. Taking his horse sharply to one side as he passed me, he said angrily: "If you want to sleep, why don't you go to the hotel and go to bed?" I did not laugh then as I was pretty keyed up, but the Irish wit of it made me laugh a lot in later years. Years afterward at some sale we were both at I told him about it and how he laughed! He was always a good race driver.

The race that day, however, was won by Fred Hyde with the mare Margaret Spangler, which is such a wonderful brood mare, now being the dam of Chief Counsel, 3, 1:57¾, King's Counsel, 1:58, and Blackstone, 4, 1:59½, all great sires at this writing. Margaret Spangler was out of Maggie Winder, 2:06½, which record was the world's pacing record for three-year-old fillies when made. Maggie Winder was sired by Oratorio, 2:13, which was the sire also of Ecstatic, 2:01¾. Fred was a very successful eastern trainer. As I recall, La Paloma got $1,000 out of the race. It was a big field and she was right in there close.

That fall she won several races. One that pleased me was the Lafayette Hotel Stake at Indianapolis. Next to her last race was late in the week at Toledo, where she won easily and then we shipped her to Lexington. We raced her early in the—week her last race of the season, and what a sparkler it was! She got her record of 2:01¾ in the second heat and the books show that she paced the last quarter in 28½ seconds. She beat a good field that day and while I was telegraphing the happy news home, in came the owner of Bessie McKlyo and said: "Well, Clair, I am sending one, too, but it is not quite as good as yours." How happy I was!

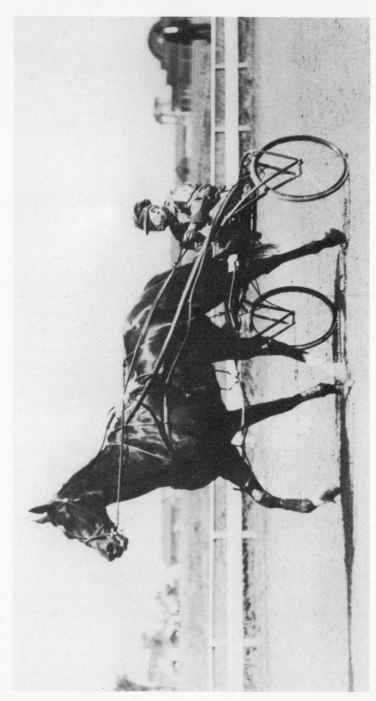

Margaret Spangler, 2:02¼, with Fred Hyde up.

Secretly I had always hoped I could win a great race over Lexington's Golden Strip. I roomed with Billy Moore in a private house, and all the angles of La Paloma's great race were gone over again and again. Finally, in the very late hours, the talk turned to the old Indiana sire which was famous when I was young, Blue Bull 75. Billy had at one time worked on one of the horse papers and had an assignment to get all the dope on the great old horse. Some of it was almost like reading a novel. I had renewed admiration for the influence Blue Bull had on Indiana horses. And what a fine little gentleman Billy was! He was the sulky salesman from Marion, Ohio. He was also very expert in taking horse pictures.

The next few days were happy ones. I heard Mr. Fox say we might go for record with La Paloma. I did not say anything, but if it had come to the showdown I would have. The sportsmanship of a horse race would have appealed to the great mare and she would have made a gallant try; but wise little old owl that she was, going to lower her record even with a runner for a pace-maker would not have caused her to make the supreme effort.

At the close of the Lexington meeting we shipped La Paloma back to Indianapolis and on Sunday the little mare which had gratified my fond hopes was led over to my home to be proudly exhibited to my family. She had put us on the map, as they say.

It was decided to ship her to the Old Glory Sale in New York that winter as she would be especially attractive to buyers for a fast class horse for the Bay State Circuit. She was kept in Indianapolis and let down and jogged until she was shipped with the different consignments of horses going to the Madison Square Sale in November. It was held at the Armory and the stalls were built in temporarily. A noisy stallion and some mares stabled near her seemed to give her the only concern I had ever seen her show. It was all strange to her and she would cuddle up to me whenever she was led out to show to a prospective buyer. She was purchased for the account of Mr. Niles of Kansas City, who maintained a summer home in Great Barrington, Massachusetts. La Paloma was put into the Walter Britenfield Stable. She had not even threatened to kick for months and all was forgiven her. As I bade farewell to the wonderful little mare I thought, of course, that it was the end of our companionship and her influence upon my life.

Mr. Fox, although a rich man, told me he used the money she brought to buy a new Stutz car. He had driven once in the Five-Hundred-Mile race at Indianapolis. He was always a very fast driver, and I had some rides with him in that Stutz that would have made your hair curl. Once after he and Max Kennedy had driven over to the races in Ohio, someone asked Max how he had come. He replied that he "flew over in Frank Fox's car." How Frank laughed when telling it!

Mr. Fox had now converted his beautiful farm for fine cattle into a trotting-horse farm and had installed as its head Peter McKlyo, later adding Braden Direct, 2:01¼, which became quite a sire himself. At the time Mr. Fox purchased Peter McKlyo, he bought several colts. He had arranged with Levi Turner to handle them out at Walter McCord's farm which had a track on it. Those who will look it up will find that Levi had been a high-class trainer who had had a long string of horses to his credit. He and Alonzo McDonald had been friends from boyhood.

One morning it had rained and Mr. Fox said to me, "You can't train horses here until after dinner. Come and go with me out to Walter's farm this morning."

As we drove in Walter was just coming in from jogging the three-year-old, Louis Direct. Mr. Fox asked Walter to let me jog him a little. As Walter handed me the lines he said: "Clair, be careful with him as I just beat 2:30 with him for the first time yesterday." I did as he requested and only jogged him a few hundred yards before I had the feeling that he was a high-class horse.

After turning the horse over to Walter I sat on the running board of Mr. Fox's car until I could catch his eye as he was always kidding with Walter. Finally he came out and I said, "Buy that horse if you can, for I have a hunch he's a high-class horse." "All right, I will try," he replied, "but you know how hard he is to deal with." I told him if we could train him until our fair he would be worth a lot of money. In a day or two he came over to my stable and told me they were leading the horse in to me from the farm. What a pacer he was!

Mr. Fox telephoned me from Cleveland ordering me to ship Louis Direct to Toledo, saying that he had a buyer for him for a lot of money. For some reason the deal didn't go through and he had me ship the horse to Kalamazoo. I was racing horses down in Indiana and was all night getting to him. I met him at breakfast and he told me to win if possible. I saw him hand a sizable sum to a very reliable owner with instructions to bet it for him.

The race was made one mile and one-eighth to avoid giving a record that would keep horses out of the stakes. We won, and I stopped for a little while before going to the stable to watch Single G. race. Like many others I was an admirer of Single G. By the time I got back to the stable Mr. Fox had sold Louis Direct for a lot of money to Walter Candler, who has owned such an array of good horses down through the years. What a fast horse he was! He ended up with a record of 1:58½, which Fred Egan had given him. In fact, Fred had him all the rest of his racing career.

I was at North Randall track and after watching Louis

Louis Direct, 1:58½, with Fred Egan up.

train, probably for sentimental reasons as much as anything, I hunted up Guy Reeder, who used to make a result
book, and bet ten dollars. I seldom bet, but I did not think
they could beat Louis Direct. Always an admirer of Egan,
who had been successful with a lot of good horses, I thought
I was in right. I was stabled in the same barn with Henry
Thomas and he and I had been good friends for years. He
confided to me that his horse had a good chance to win as
he had brushed his horse an eighth in 13½ seconds. I
thought maybe I had better "take out a little insurance,"
as they say. I hunted Guy up again and this time bet ten
on Henry's horse. We were to race at Toledo the following
week and I rode up to Kalamazoo with good old George
Loomis and his wife. She sensed that I was having a lot of
fun listening to her kid George. I can't think back over
any trip I enjoyed as much. We talked about everything
and he confided to me that he had bet $150 in the result
book on Hollyrood Walter in his stable. Horsemen were
agreed that George was a "loner" when it came to telling
anybody about a horse he was going to put over. Here I was
with information I knew was "hot from the feedbox." I
hunted Guy up yet again and bet ten more on George's
horse to cover up the twenty I had bet on the other two.

Come race day Henry won the first heat with Hollyrood
Volo, Fred won the second heat with Louis Direct, and
George won the third and fourth heats and race with Hollyrood Walter. I ended up winner of about $80, and if either
one of the other horses had won it would have been the
same. Anyhow I had a lot of fun trying to bet on the right
horse.

The next summer after we sold La Paloma, I went over
to the stable one morning and one of the boys told me she
was over in a box car. Mr. Fox had been up to the Bay
State Circuit and had told Mr. Niles to ship her back to me.

Single G, 1:58½, with Ed Allen up.

Not only had I not been consulted, but I did not even know she was coming.

I started on her again and she was really tough this time. After I got her so so I could repeat her a little, I shipped her over to the Muncie fair and won the first heat with her. She got beaten but paced a beautiful race. I had not realized how short of work she had really been, as there had been little correspondence.

On that Muncie trip George Loomis confessed to me that he had an ambition to win the Kalamazoo derby and also to drive a trotter in two minutes. He thought he had such a trotter in his stable then in a mare called Minia Dillon, which had a record of 2:02½. He had given the pacer Sir Roch a record of 1:59¼. Sir Roch used to hit his knees and George used those little calks that screw into the shoe such as are used on horses that race over the ice. It worked on Sir Roch and was really great handling on the part of George. He raced a lot of horses good in his career.

The next week I shipped La Paloma to an old mile track in Rockport down in southern Indiana. This was the first and only time I was ever on a race track where I knew only one man. He was John F. Jones. La Paloma was the worst I ever saw her that day. To add to my uneasiness, Mrs. Wolverton was in the hospital expecting to give birth to our fourth child.

There was no center field fence and La Paloma was stabled on the far side. Being a small field that day, we tried to time it so that when the others had taken a couple of scores, I could mount and hustle her away on her first appearance down there. There was one thing about her, she would always race perfectly in a field of horses. The groom, a veteran saddle-horse man, conceived the idea of giving her her first warming-up heat under saddle. I gave her the other two heats to a training cart, and how she would kick! I can see her yet being led across that center field. Whenever she bounced against the kicking strap she would raise that sulky way up over her back, and she would do it several times whenever she came out for a heat.

There was a nice crowd that day with a good many big young fellows in it who looked to me as if they would fight if aroused. Being a believer in the maxim that "discretion is the better part of valor," I was trying to be very careful what I said and to whom. They all seemed to be very interested in the mare. Of course, they had suggestions about handling one like her. I was very careful to listen because one never knows when or where a good idea is going to come. I was afraid that the caretaker's lack of tact and also his being a little nervous over the mare might make him say something that would get us both beaten up. Naturally I supposed the crowd would be on the side of the local horses.

I won the first heat and in the second I was trying to save her all I could. I was in front as we turned into the stretch. The horse behind me pulled out right quickly and over in front of me, spoiling any chance I had. In so doing he had broken a rule we all know. There was no flag up and of course they were two-timing me plenty. The mare was not really up to much as I realized by then. I was a little angry and went to the judges' stand and said, "Gentlemen, you know the rules and you saw what happened." They replied, "Yes, we know and have been watching one take you while the other laid up a-plenty. You go on down and we will take care of it." As I went down out of the stand there stood one of those big husky young fellows. He wanted to know about it and while I was telling him, they announced that La Paloma had been given the heat. He said to me, "That's a good thing they did that for there is a bunch of us boys here that would have pushed this judges' stand over." I really believe they would have done it, too.

It proved again that Americans, wherever they are, like their sports, but the winner must win on the square.

The mare was getting leg-tired by now. We went the full five heats and she had to take second money. I was all night getting back to Indianapolis. When I arrived at the hospital early the next morning I learned that George had been born late that night. George, like the others, knows a great deal about horses. Mrs. Wolverton and I have had wonderful pleasure with him. Wasn't I richly rewarded for taking such a chance?

Mr. Niles had written me, in answer to a letter and a telegram from Muncie, with a nice offer to race La Paloma's remaining stakes in the Bay State Circuit. I wrote I could not accept owing to the obligations I felt to the other owners, but that if there were any races in his country after I was through here I would bring her at the regular price. Well, she was getting tightened up a little more all the time and at Converse, Indiana, she won a heat and kept another good mare pretty busy beating her in a free-for-all pace.

Then for her last race of the year we shipped her to Mr. Niles' summer home, Great Barrington, Massachusetts. He was such a nice man. He came around and asked me to race her to a training cart instead of a sulky as he feared she might kick me. I told him no, that I had been racing her to a sulky and I was pretty sure I would get along all right. They started another horse in the same race. He won and I was second with La Paloma. I will always think she could have beaten him easily.

To her credit let me say that her manners were perfect and she was safe as a church in the progress of racing a heat. It was when she was warming up or jogging or coming back from a false score that she might kick.

She was shipped back to Indiana after Mr. Niles arranged with me to leave her with me for another year. He made me a nice present and I went on down to Lexington. La Paloma got pretty good-mannered again that winter.

Chapter IV

THE PASSING OF LA PALOMA

I WAS getting a new friend and we are still friends— Jack Karstedt and also his good wife. I raced Twinkling Belle, 2:04¾, for him a couple of years. She came to me a terrific puller. A former friend and patron had sent me over from Lafayette the year before a big three-year-old chestnut gelding which we later named Purdue after the university in West Lafayette. I liked his breeding. He was sired by William, 1:58½, his dam was by Walter Direct, 2:05¾. Twinkling Belle took a liking to the big gelding and we got to training them together late that winter and early spring. I kept working her trailing him until she learned to trail a horse and quit pulling. One day, just for fun, I took her out from behind him and she went by him like you would throw a baseball. Discovering what she had done, she actually took up and waited for him. We noted, too, that she liked to be near the chestnut horse when out grazing. Don't tell me these horses don't have their friendships!

Also I raced Dorothy Nixon for Mr. Karstedt. She was a good two-year-old for me, winning at Muncie and getting the Indiana 2:12 record for the season for two-year-old pacers.

After the racing season was over the year Twinkling

73

Walter Dear, 3, 2:02¾ with Walter Cox driving.

Belle performed so creditably, Mr. Karstedt made us a present of a car, the first we ever owned. What a lot of pleasure it gave us with our four little children!

When Purdue came to me the year before, I asked Jim Odom, who had brought him over for the man, if he had any speed. He said, "Why, Clair, that colt can pace like a hog falling down a well." Of course, that got a laugh out of me as he had intended. I will always believe that training those two horses together helped them both. Those who look it up will find that Twinkling Belle won several races and beat some pretty fair horses with some "smart cookies" driving them. We won an odd distance race with her at Cleveland that year and the next morning a nice big car drove up and the man in it said, "What kind of rigging did he have on that mare? She warmed up like a crazy mare last year." Cliff, the caretaker, was cleaning her bridle and showed it to him—a little open bridle with a plain snaffle bit. Afterwards he laughed when he told me the man acted as if he were being "taken for a ride."

Purdue was not so fast, but I gave him a half-mile track record of 2:09½, and won a stake with him and got him sold to a patron of Ed Allen, who raced him good for quite a while.

Rose Marie Abbe, 2:00½, raced creditably for me as a three-year-old and I gave her a record of 2:03¼ that year. I just got her beaten by a whisker in 2:01½ at Indianapolis by a big chestnut mare Doc Parshall was driving. She beat Colonel Strong at Lexington and he had beaten her at Charleston, Illinois, earlier that season. Mr. T. J. Stahl, who owned Colonel Strong, was in a kidding mood the day before we raced and entertained a group of us nearly all afternoon up in the grandstand. That race at Lexington got her sold and she went on and raced good for several seasons. J. B. McCord and Alvah Crouch owned her while I raced

Rodney, 1:57¾, with Bi Shively up.

her. Mr. Crouch is dead, but J.B., who is a conductor on the Monon Railroad, still comes around in company with Ernest Mockford. They are both good friends of mine and I enjoy them. All of us call J.B. "Monon" and I suspect a good many of the boys don't know his real name.

Another horse that raced good for me was Ora Main, 2:04¼. I gave him his record at Columbus, Ohio. I always thought he was quite a little faster than the record I gave him.

Horsemen are pretty well agreed that Walter Cox was one of our very great trainers and drivers. His reputation, too, for wit and repartee was outstanding and nearly everyone remembers some of the things he said. They tell this one: Cox and Dick McMahon were sitting under their awning the next day after they had given big Roy Owen a pretty hard time of it with a trotter called Tommy Horn. Roy was still mad and as he passed them he said, "I am on my way to the train home, but I have still got time to lick both of you." After he was out of earshot and nothing had happened, Cox turned to Dick and said, "You are in an awful shape, aren't you?"

Ed Allen, here out of the West, could take care of himself pretty well with Cox or anybody else. He and Cox were good friends and I have had many a hearty laugh at the things they said to each other. It was through Ed that Cox bought the great trotter, Mabel Trask, 2:01¾. The contests that she and Saint Frisco had, with Mr. Geers driving Frisco, were real thrillers.

Another driver of that same era was Curt Gosnell of Cambridge City, Indiana. He and Cox were also good friends. Like Cox he was known for his wit. If one will look up the horses he raced successfully it will be understood why we Hoosiers admired him. After Howard Vickory had brought out the great Single G. and raced him a little, Curt took over and raced him until Curt's death. Single G. won the much coveted Chamber of Commerce Pacing Stake.

Walter Cox, Ed Allen, and Curt Gosnell have all passed on, but another with a keen sense of humor is still living—Bion Shively. You have only to mention the name Bi and every horseman knows whom you mean. He has always raced horses successfully, but his success has been outstanding with Rodney, The Colonel's Lady, and lately with the Hambletonian winner, Sharp Note. Bi has been aptly called the Will Rogers of the Trotting Turf. I wonder who has not been kidded by him as he knows everybody who has been around harness horses. Even knowing I will run second, I still cannot resist the temptation to say something to him just for the fun of hearing the kidding I am sure to get. Wouldn't it have been fun to have had Bi, Ed Allen, Cox and Curt together some rainy afternoon? I believe I would still want a ticket on Bi. I spent one such afternoon with Arlie Frost, who was a great friend of Bi. He could imitate him to perfection and the stories he told of him were sidesplitting. Arlie was a nice fellow, very bright, and raced horses very successfully.

At different times over a long period of years I trained horses for Mr. O. A. Jose, owner of Josedale Farms. A closeup will reveal that the Josedale horses have raced well all over the country. Counterpart Maid was a very fast mare for two or three of us trainers. I had her last and how she raced that year until an accident finished her career!

Josedale Leader was the champion gelding two-year-old of the year, getting a record of 2:08 over the Louisville half-mile track. He beat a really good field that day, among them one that two years later paced in 1:59½.

Josedale Director, an older full brother, I believe was a possible two-minute pacer had it been elected to race him without hopples and over good mile tracks. As I recall, we gave him a record of 2:06½ over a half-mile track. Josedale Hoosier also raced well and I gave him a record of 2:07½. Mr. Jose seemed to have a great liking for him.

Everybody liked P. J. Kennedy of Templeton, Indiana. Pat did not have to take his hat off or push it back to hook his glasses over his ears. He drove his own horses for years, and successfully, too. He was a good judge of a trotter and managed his horses well. The last good horse he owned was the trotter Linworthy, 2:02¼. Pat died before this one reached his greatest form. His estate, of which his son Paul was the executor, raced him the following year. In most of his races he had been driven by Walter Dispanette, who, by the way, is pretty good with anybody's horse. For some reason Walter did not come to Rensselaer, Indiana, and I was invited to drive him. He beat a good field there and the following week I won with him at Indianapolis, beating a good field of trotters, and gave him his present record of 2:02¼. I followed with wins at Kentland and Bourbon in Indiana and Hillsdale in Michigan. At Hillsdale he defeated a good trotter in the horse Ankabar, 2:01½, which had not lost a race that season over a half-mile track. He won his last heat and should have won his last race that fall at Ottawa, Ohio.

Linworthy was bred at Josedale Farm and sold as a colt to someone around the track at Indianapolis. P. J. bought him cheap, recognizing a good trotter in him. He corrected a few of his faults and here he came, racing for years afterwards.

The following year, after I got La Paloma back from Great Barrington, I got her to race again. She was not nearly so much trouble to train. I raced her a few times, and as I remember, she paced in 2:05, separately timed at Kalamazoo. Her legs, however, were beginning to look a little suspicious. Mr. Niles then sold her back to Mr. Fox and the next year her career as a brood mare began. Her first foal was Palomita, 2:07, on a half-mile track.

Mr. P. C. Isaacs had become one of my patrons by now. He was a fine owner and a former patron of the great trainer Charley Dean, and also of his son Chase Dean, who has been successful over the years. A year or two after Charley's death, at Joe Markey's suggestion, he came to me. He had owned the wonderful horse Minor Heir, 1:58½, before becoming my patron.

When the filly, La Paloma's first foal, was old enough to wean, Mr. Isaac said to me: "I know you want to train her and I am going to buy her for you."

Joe Markey was a fine harness horse scribe and I used to love to read his articles in the *Horse Review*, the paper on which he had worked for many years. Knowing that he had served in the Spanish-American War and very likely knew the meaning of Spanish words, I wrote to him and asked him to suggest a name synonymous with La Paloma. He came up with Palomita which means "little dove."

Down through the years I have made a hobby of naming horses with which I was connected when I had the opportunity. Among them was Turk McGlory, 2:13¼, Tarquin, Foremost, 2:07¼, Shiloh, 2:10, La Paloma, 2:01¾, Gahagan, 2:10, Arizona, 2:06⅗, Anton Lang, 2:00½, Carty Nagle, 2:00, Panama, 2:09¼. The mare Her Ladyship, 1:56¾, I had named Allegra, but after selling her to Mr. Jackson he decided to change her name. Therefore I wrote in to the register and received permission to use the name Allegra again, this time on a mare which did not stand training, so we put her to breeding. Her first colt Gahagan, 2:10, got his record in that part of Canada where it takes a good horse to go that fast. The next filly Arizona, 2:06⅗, paced a race in 1954 in 2:04. Still Waters, 2:05½, was another that I named. My latest is the sucking filly Ante

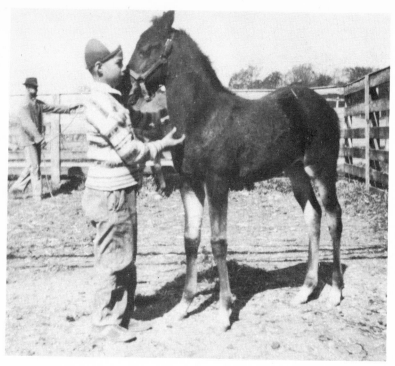

La Paloma's foal Palomita.

Bellum, sired by Jimmy Creed, 1:59⅘, her dam Allegra.

There was another foal I named—Quick Quaker—and perhaps this is as good a place as any to tell of another experience. Selma Lenore, named after our only daughter, was bought by a Belgian. He paid a hundred dollars on her seven-hundred-dollar price. He bought some other horses, too, to ship to Belgium. Then the man literally dropped out of sight. As I went about I heard much criticism of him. Men who had sold him horses but had never been paid called him a crook. Somehow I didn't worry about the money he owed me on Selma Lenore.

I made a trip to Lexington and when I came home, as I was approaching the house, two children hailed me with: "You'll have some good news when you get home."

And I did. In my absence the Belgian had come to our home and paid Mrs. Wolverton the remaining six hundred dollars. He said he had fallen on the street in Detroit, ill from typhoid fever, and had just gotten out of the hospital.

Selma Lenore was out of a crippled mare by Sydney Dillon, which, in turn, was out of Saralma, the dam of Pan Michael, 2:03¼ pacing and 2:12¼ trotting, which was the one-time champion double-gaited horse. Saralma was also the dam of Boralma, 2:07, owned by Thomas W. Lawson, a millionaire sportsman. Boralma, it will be remembered, won the Kentucky Futurity and figured in one of the great match races.

The Belgian never shipped Selma Lenore home. Instead he put her on the Josedale Stock Farm and left her. Mr.

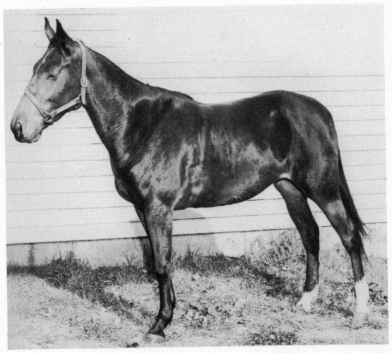

Arizona, by Royal Napoleon out of Allegra.

Pen sketch of Still Waters 2:05½.

Jose bred her to Peter Lincoln. The foal, which was Quick Quaker, was bought by Mr. Isaacs and turned over to me. I trained him along with Palomita and several others.

We had entered Palomita at Lexington, but she had gotten hurt and we did not take her. I made a joking remark that I was going to take Quick Quaker to Lexington if I had to walk and lead him.

After arriving it looked to be foolish to start him as supposedly he was in too deep. Knowing, however, that Mr. Isaacs had to pay the dead entry on Palomita anyway, I finally decided to start him in the Kentucky Stake.

It was misting that day and the track got heavier and heavier. I began to drive carefully, hoping to save the entry fee and ended up by winning the third heat. My friends and I were very excited and saw now that I had a chance to win. My stop watch had gone bad and I borrowed

Goose Bay 3, 2:00⅔, with Jakie Mahoney driving.

another before the fourth heat, intending to trot Quick Quaker fast enough to keep the brush out of the contending mare Pocahantas. But however, the borrowed watch failed, too. Once on the track I made the mistake of trying to save Quick Quaker and left it to a brush, Pocahantas out-trotted me.

I had a pleasant train ride that night from Lexington to Cincinnati with Aaron Williams, owner of Pocahantas. Pocahantas will be remembered as one of the very great mares on the Walnut Hall Farm, being the dam of Indian Land, 1:59⅘.

But to return to La Paloma. Her next foal died a few hours after foaling. That spring Mr. Fox decided to sell all his horses. When La Paloma came into the sales ring I bid her off for my very own, probably the luckiest thing I ever did. When I took her out of the sales barn, I engaged a truck and took her to Dick Granger's farm and bred her to Single G. The resultant foal was Still Waters, 2:05½, which became a wonderful brood mare in her own right. In her last years of racing she was reputed to have paced an eighth in 13½ seconds during one of her workouts. I raced her as a two-year-old without hopples and she paced in 2:07, and in one of her races she paced the last quarter in 30 seconds.

La Paloma's next foal died at foaling time. We were all at the stall when the little colt died and noticed La Paloma nosed straw over her little dead foal, then leaving it alone. She was then rebred to Single G. and produced Panama, 2:09.

And speaking of Panama—what a good race horse with enduring qualities he was for years! When he was eighteen I saw him win a heat at Old Orchard. Joe Eyler told me that he had raced him in his younger years when he thought he could pace in 2:03 over a good mile track. I named him

Phantom Lady 3, 1:58⅗, driven by Frank Ervin.

Panama after a motion picture I took my family to see because of a comedian I saw in it.

While Panama was at La Paloma's side, I sent her to Village Farm, which was owned by Gage Ellis, and bred her to Abbedale, the result being Her Ladyship, 1:56¾, the world's champion pacing mare. Her Ladyship is the dam of Goose Bay 3, 2:00⅖, a nice individual to look at and a great money winner and now a successful sire. Splendid success that he was, however, I find myself wishing that an attempt had been made after he was thoroughly gaited in hopples to train him without hopples and shadow roll by some trainer like Mr. Geers, who would not drive a hopple pacer. Knowing the family as I do, who is to know how fast he might have paced? I once timed Her Ladyship a quarter in 28½ seconds without hopples. I belong to the few who believe that, everything else being equal, a good free-legged pacer can beat a good hopple pacer.

The aggregate sale of Her Ladyship's produce through the auctions is stupendous. I, for one, believe that the $55,000 paid for Gosling will be justified. However undoubtedly her greatest foal was Phantom Lady 3, 1:58⅗ which was raced so successfully by Frank Ervin for her owner Mrs. H. Willis Nichols, Jr., of Walnut Hall Farm at Donerail, Ky.

La Paloma's next foal was Carty Nagle, 2:00. I liked the sound of the name but had never met Mr. Nagle who, Johnny Dickerson told me, was a saddle-horse man and quite a character and story teller. I raced Carty Nagle as a two-year-old and I can think back with pleasure on that. Times were a little tough just then and I thought it might save a little to let my small sons take care of him through each race. It really looked cute to see Ken leading, and George following the sulky to the track, Carty Nagle raced

Carty Nagle (Tom Berry) defeats the $500,000 Adios in 2:00 at Old Orchard, Maine.

Carty Nagle (Tom Berry) winning the first heat of the free-for-all pace at Lexington, Ky., from King's Counsel, 1:58; Adios, 1:57½; and Little Pat, 1:58¾.

Her Ladyship, 1:56¾.

good for me and that winter I sold him to the people who were in some way connected with the Fords of Detroit. He won all of his races that season. Since Ken and George were so very interested, we provided them with expense money and they boarded a train headed for Ionia, Michigan. I had written my good friend Jim Adams to keep an eye on them. The Michigan people were very kind to them. Carty won and those two youngsters came home happy, giving us a vivid description of the race. We have always been glad we arranged for them to go.

I did not see it, but it must have been a funny sight. The previous fall, after the racing season was over, one Saturday afternoon Ken decided to jog Carty. For some reason he hitched him to a sulky instead of a cart. He was wearing a derby hat someone had discarded. Homer Walton saw it and laughed about it and thought it cute.

Carty, the Detroit owners feeling he was "through" at the end of his three-year-old form, was later sold to Mr. Bowman Brown, Publisher of *The Harness Horse,* a paper very popular with horse lovers. He raced wonderfully for Mr. Brown, taking his present record. He was retired to Mr. Brown's farm, where I doubt very much if a horse could occupy a warmer spot in his owner's heart. Mrs. Wolverton and I were attending the Harrisburg Sale and Mr. Brown provided us with transportation up to his farm some little distance away to see Carty Nagle. If ever a horse lives the life of Riley it is he. He has a nice warm, clean box stall at night, and a fine pasture, with even an old horse for companionship, for the day. Needless to say we hold Mr. Brown in affectionate regard.

Two unsuccessful attempts were made to get La Paloma in foal to Grattan Bars, and I had made arrangements to send her the next day to be bred to Dick Reynolds. Then Mr. Leo McNamara came to my home with a contract to breed the great mare to Two Gaits Farm stallions during her remaining years, with a special proviso that at her death she was to have a careful burial there on the farm. He lived up to his contract to the letter, thereby endearing himself in our sentimental hearts probably more than he suspects. He occupies a very important role in the welfare of the trotting-horse business. The doings at his great breeding farm and the success of the colts bred there are always a source of pleasure to me.

It seemed that each time it became necessary to furnish funds to send one of the Wolvertons to college, the money came from the sale of one of La Paloma's colts. I used to say laughingly that in the past indulgence in race horses

Grattan Bars, 1:59½, on the right, Winnipeg, 1:57¾, on the left.

may have kept some children from attaining college educations, yet in our case La Paloma actually furnished the money.

Even those of our neighbors, friends, and relatives who did not care for horses knew the important role this mare played in our lives. At her passing I wrote a little article and had a few printed to give to friends who I thought would appreciate that kind of thing and am hereby appending it:

THE PASSING OF LA PALOMA

I had known all that winter that La Paloma was growing very feeble and on Saturday night about April 1st a telephone call from Two Gaits Farm, advised me that the end was very near. The next day Mrs. Wolverton and I drove to the farm; and as it was noon, the help was away to dinner. I finally found her stall and in opening the door, I heard a low call and there lay the brave little friend who had done so much for the Wolvertons. The Master of Two Gaits Farm had seen to it that everything possible was done to care for her. Good shelter, plenty of bedding and every kind of feed prepared to help her keep her strength. But her teeth had become so bad that she was unable to chew her food, and together with the inexorable demands of age and the constant drain of foaling and sucking foals she had now come to the end.

I entered her stall and sat down in the straw near her head. She was calmly waiting the call of the grim messenger on the gray horse—asking no quarter, and giving none, just as she had always done with her adversaries on the race track. Death, death that terrorizes the very young and is tragedy to those in the full bloom of health and success, but is a boon provided

by an all-wise Creator to release the aged and failing
in strength from the unequal struggle. But as I sat
there looking into the brave eyes and stroking the
sensitive ears and nice forehead, I did not think of the
wasted little form, but instead my thoughts went back
to that glorious afternoon in Lexington when she was
in her youth so unusually well muscled for one of her
height and so bounteously supplied by nature with
nerve and vitality, she had come finishing at terrific
speed the race which was to make her glorious, and to
realize for me a boyhood dream that some day I might
be privileged to win a great race on a Grand Circuit
track from Grand Circuit drivers. Even those nearest
and dearest to me do not fully realize how much I love
the profession of driving harness races and how I
craved a little success. Only a privileged few who loved
their profession could possibly understand. My mind
toyed with the happiness I had in the telegraph office
preparing the message of joyful news to my loved ones.
I thought again of the cherished compliment I received that day from a great horseman who was sincere and really knew. Lived over again that night too
happy to sleep. Sharing a room with a friend, a great
horseman, talking until the wee small hours of the
morning about the great horses of other days he had
known. One of them in particular, a great sire appearing in her pedigree. As I sat there I thought again of
our racing career together and believed we understood
each other. Thought of that fall after the great race,
of how the bidders at the New York Sale had striven
with one another to be her owner. Thought of how
when her racing days were ended, and her owner decided to dispose of all his horses, that I, through senti-

ment, had gone in debt to buy her and how that was blessed.

She generously passed on to her foals her own great strength and vitality—one of her foals is the world's champion pacing mare; others of them great race horses. Like their mother, none of them trained brilliantly. But when it came to racing, they put forth their best in true sportsman-like manner, challenging one and all. I thought of how the sale of her foals had provided money for the family to educate fine boys and a lovely girl; how we all loved and appreciated her and what she had made possible.

Her name was always spoken with gratitude and respect in our family. As I sat there I saw her again, that beautiful bay mare, perfectly gaited, sometimes stormy, always misunderstood by the public who believed she was mean and sour at heart. We were more than race horse and trainer. We were friends and understood each other.

Her mission is completed. She died without pain and peacefully, her name known to every informed horseman. Knowing this was the last time I would see my little equine friend alive, I took my leave, feeling a very humbled debtor.

I had many chances to sell her which would have been considered no more quickly than I would have considered selling one of the family.

I was anxious that her last days would be spent in a good home and part of the contract with Two Gaits Farm was that at her death she should be buried on the farm and not be hauled away to a fertilizing plant. She died that night, and the next day the farm help and I dug a grave on a little hillside. We put straw in the bottom and hauled her to the grave and placed

The passing of La Paloma.

her in, careful to lay her head and limbs comfortably, and covered her over with a nice blanket before filling the grave with dirt.

La Paloma, I know where you're sleeping. In the spring I like to think that your spirit is hovering about beautiful Two Gaits fields, among the wild flowers, birds, and bees; that you see the little foals playing, some of them destined to do great things on the race tracks. Again, I think of you in the sky soaring through space. Perchance you will meet the mythical winged Pegasus. If you do, please tell him of the little Indiana family that loved you and thinks gratefully on you. Tell him that they, in their fierce loyalty, would bet a little that even he could not beat you in a sprint across the sky.

Brave little mare, did you know me that last time I came to you? I like to think so.

CHAPTER V

PEOPLE, HORSES, AND SOME MEMORIES

ALWAYS I have felt a warm friendship for Walter McCord, and for his good wife who has lately passed on. Walter was "hit with the club of common sense" and his success with horses is in no way an accident. His winter and spring method of jogging and preparing horses is very like that of Walter Cox, and I find myself wondering if a great part of his success did no come from that. The triumphs of horses which he has bred, owned, and trained is outstanding. In a reminiscent mood he told me of a Blue Bull stallion he owned that was really the foundation of this wonderful line of horses he has bred. He tells me that in the old days he could leave this horse in a tie stall for thirty days, then take him out and he would pace an eighth in 15 seconds and that once he timed him an eighth in 12½ seconds. Like many horses of his day he contracted distemper and it left his wind affected. Some smart guy from Chicago heard of him and bought him to win a short match race. We never heard of him afterwards.

Even a cat can look at a king. Wouldn't I like to live to see the result of the blending of these two families which have inherited so much extreme speed on the maternal side —Myrtle McKlyo, 2:00½, and La Paloma, 2:01¾! Think what might happen if the Hal Dale mare Walter is now

racing were bred to Goose Bay, or one of the mares out of
La Paloma or Her Ladyship were bred to Jimmy Creed!

We breed beautifully gaited trotters. Then why cannot
we breed steady-going pacers if we select mares which for
two or three generations have adopted the pacing gait, and
mate them with stallions which have pacing inheritance?
Add to this the starting gate which allows horses to get
nicely on their stride. Of course it is not true of all of them,
but are not many of our horses racing in hopples that would
race free-legged if given a chance? What might have been
the result if Harry Pownall had not had for an owner Mr.
Harriman, who, I am told, does not race hopple pacers?
Differently handled the great mare Tassel Hanover, 1:57⅘,
might have been just another fussy hopple pacer. None of
La Paloma's foals, with the exception of Carty Nagle—and
I am told he could pace a quarter better than 30 seconds
free legged—ever paced a step until they were in harness.
Then before they had gone a quarter of a mile they would
slip over into a nice pace. Tell me there is nothing in inheritance! Ed Avery, who was Lon McDonald's wonderful
second trainer and friend, had, at my invitation, just driven
Carty Nagle, then just a little over a year old, an eighth in
18¼ seconds and made this statement: "Isn't it funny
trainers will patiently work with a trotting colt, but let a
pacing colt make a break and they will outfit him with hopples right away." Lon McDonald would not drive a hopple
pacer. He had a little mare which had worn hopples, but
he shod her differently and outfitted her with a pair of toe
weights and raced her successfully, giving her a record of
2:04¼. Lon McDonald was a fine gentleman as well as a
very skilled horseman.

I was always a great admirer of Lady Maud C., 2:00½,
and of Hedgewood Boy, 2:01. Who knows but what the
mare had a marked influence on the success of the great

Adios? But for his death I had intended to breed La Paloma to Hedgewood Boy following her mating with Single G. I can see him yet walking in parade, one of the most unusually muscled horses I ever saw. One's mind in a flight of fancy could picture him as a Norseman marching majestically at the head of his clan, leading them into battle.

Dick McMahon beat him one fall over at Columbus with Citation, affectionately known around the stable as Sadie, but to the credit of Al Sweet, who raced Hedgewood Boy

Calumet Butler 3, 2:02½, with Dick McMahon doing the driving.

that season, he seemed to be going very good-gaited. He always raced well for all his trainers. A pretty successful sire, he might have made a truly great showing if he had been on one of the big stock farms.

The ever-increasing number of women interested in this sport is pleasing, for they are adding refinement and dignity to it. At Orlando, Florida, one can see men who have achieved prominence in the business world sitting with their wives enjoying the morning workouts. The knowledge many women have about harness horses is gratifying. For instance, the Grady sisters have a wide acquaintance with horse lovers, and their information about horses and their doings is remarkable. Mrs. Wolverton and I think the Grady sisters can do about anything. We wonder if they could prevail on Ireland's patron saint, Saint Patrick, to make a flying trip over here to Florida and banish the snakes as he did in Ireland.

There are several women driving races now and doing a clever, brainy job of it, too. One winter recently when I was in Florida I noticed Mary Louise McGregor, who can do a lot of things. She helps her husband train, drives a skillful horse race, writes a column of horse news, and takes pictures for the horse papers.

I am, of course, a little partial, but after seeing Mrs. Ora Dunkin drive Her Ladyship a very fast workout, I would have to say she is a very fine reinswoman. She just naturally knows a lot about the harness horses. Her husband is quite successful in the sulky, and Mrs. Wolverton and I are both fans of their son, Thomas.

Mrs. Greeley Winings is another lady who can think without anybody's help. She has made quite a place for herself among the admirers of harness horses. I was over at Cleveland and it was she who first called my attention to Tommy Berry's ability. Her husband was a very well-

known man in this sport and the very able manager of
Laurel Hall Farm, with Peter the Great, the wonder sire,
at its head. The owner was Stoughton Fletcher.

Greeley Winings and Stoughton A. Fletcher occupied a
prominent place in harness horse affairs for several years.
It seemed to me that Greeley could go on any race track, be
it Grand Circuit or a half-mile track, and in a short time be
enjoying the confidence of the most important people. If
anybody had a horse he thought he would bet on, Greeley
was generally in on the know. Very often he would do the
betting for the person. He was very alert mentally. I never
knew any fellow quite like him. He once told me that the
money paid for the wonder stallion Peter the Great was
won by the betting he had done that season for Mr.
Fletcher. Greeley bet a lot of money for him and they went
places in the betting ring. It took a great deal of nerve to
pay $50,000 for Peter the Great at twenty-one years old,
but the results prove what a sound investment it was. Just
think of the great horses which were bred there! Among
the last was Elizabeth, the dam of our world's champion
Greyhound. Greeley was a great manager for the farm and
when the Peter the Greats went into the sales ring in
New York they attracted much attention. It was said Mr.
Fletcher used to come home from the bank and spend hours
under the trees in the pasture enjoying the young colts.

"Jakey" Councilman took care of Peter the Great and
the attachment between horse and man was beautiful. The
old horse passed on a few years ahead of "Jakey," but at
the latter's death he requested that his body be cremated
and that George Gahagan scatter his ashes over the grave
of the great horse that is buried there at the farm.

Mrs. Harry Whitney and Mrs. Frank Ervin both play
very important roles in the success of their famous husbands. Billy Marvin used to tell me his daughter Lou could

really drive a horse. She married Charles Dunkin, another member of the Dunkin family. Again, Mrs. Dennis Shell and Mrs. Charles McGown are really significant factors in the triumphs of their husbands. Both seem to have a knack about caring for horses and their judgment on the chances of a young prospect was better than fair.

Besides the ones I know but cannot now recall, there are many more who add to the good of the sport. Women who first came just for the companionship of their husbands are now enjoying a nice clean recreation. It is surprising how well they like the horses and how informed they are. The time is not far distant when there will be as many women sponsoring harness horses as there are women sponsoring runners.

With the exception of Mary Louise McGregor and the Grady sisters, all these women I have mentioned are, I am proud to say, products of Indiana.

And speaking of Indiana, due to the horse interest and the fact that several of the state's prominent horsemen came from that locality, Rushville has been called the "Lexington of Indiana." Most people of that era were agreed that Dick Wilson was one of our very top Grand Circuit drivers. Along with his brother Samp, who, it was said, was an expert balancer and conditioner of their horses, he made their stable one to be reckoned with at the races. Aileen Wilson, 2:03¼, was one of theirs.

Jack Curry, a colorful Grand Circuit driver years ago, trained at the Rushville track at least one season. He raced the one-time champion, sweet little Alix, 2:03¾, for the greater part of her career, winning the famous Columbian free-for-all. He also raced the grey trotting gelding Serpol, 2:10.

Among others training at Rushville were the Dagler boys, John, Clate and Will. All were successful at racing horses. Their father stood the stallion Ess. H. Kay, 2:00¾, there for a while. Cas Johnston, a resident of Rushville, trained there a great deal.

Indiana's own Harrie Jones, a lifetime resident of Rush-ville, earlier in his career trained a big stable of horses there and achieved success with them, too. Among them was the blind grey pacing stallion New Richmond, 2:07¼, and later was Alcyfras, 2:03¾. Harrie had a knack in handling a horse that was a little fussy. Later in life he acted as secretary of our Indiana Trotting and Pacing Horse Association. He was also secretary to the sales com-pany of Palin and Winings and took a very active part in the racing interests at the Indiana State Fair.

I believe Luke W. Duffy spent his last years in Rush-ville. He owned a good little half-mile track trotter during that time. I raced horses a little for him and his brother Elam and enjoyed being around them.

There were, in fact, quite a number of people around Rushville who were interested in horses. Those mentioned are only a few.

I like to think of the pleasant hours I spent with Bob Smith, who had a wide acquaintance. He was an excellent fellow to visit with and his stories of famous horsemen and their doings were always entertaining. He was a good judge of a horse and the latter part of his life was spent in ex-porting horses to New Zealand, where he had friends. He sent quite a few horses which raced good in that country.

As I understand it, he liked to drive a horse and did it well. He spotted the mare Sweet Marie, got her under lease, took her East and raced her very successfully that season. She was a high class mare and wound up a year or two later with a record of 2:02 in Alta McDonald's hands.

Bob was a great friend and admirer of William Durfee, who was, perhaps, the greatest California trainer, and who raced successfully in the East. I understand that Durfee's father, also a trainer, raced the stallion McKinney, 2:11¼, and gave him his record. We are all aware what a great influence descendants of McKinney play in our present-day horses.

Speaking of California trainers, there was Charles Witt, who trained and first invaded the Grand Circuit with the S. A. Camp Stable, which now is one of our most prominent stables.

There will always be plenty of room in this world for Bob Smith's kind. Both he and Will Durfee have passed on, but they both counted for a lot in the horse business.

I remember a conversation between Greeley Winings and Bob Smith about the old days. They told about seeing George Starr drive Direct, 2:05½, to a high-wheeled sulky a quarter in 27¾ seconds at Cambridge City, Indiana. Thus one can see they had extreme speed even in those days. Is it not probable that the betting meetings, dash racing, and greater number of places to race—thus making it possible to race perhaps three or four times as many horses as used to be raced—explain in part, at least, why we have many more horses now that can go exceedingly fast, especially the two-year-olds? Add to all these factors the greater number of standard crosses, plus more efficacious feeding and growing on the part of our stock farms.

It seems to me that the added crosses have evolved more of a type of standard-bred than we used to have. They now look as distinctive as does the thoroughbred. The improved type and gait make it much easier to balance and train a trotter than formerly. Our trotters and pacers alike both come from the same families of speed inheritance. One often finds that in members of the same family one will have his best record on the trot and the other on the pace. And again, many horses will take records at both gaits.

Instead of getting pacers as more or less of a by-product from horses we hoped would be trotters, why not try to breed pacers that are naturally as good-gaited and safe as are some of our trotters of today? Why couldn't one select stallions which got their best records on the pace and the sires and dams of which had been pacers, and breed mares to them the best records of which were on the pace, and include as many pacing crosses thereafter as possible? I have already mentioned that Mr. Geers and Lon McDonald would not drive hopple pacers. Yet they gave to the sport some really great pacers. Probably he was joking, but I remember that Harry Whitney, in speaking of Nibble Hanover, said, "You guys up in Indiana would have had a hopple pacer out of that horse." While truth is ofttimes spoken in jest, that is just about what would have happened. Nibble Hanover is siring quite a few good pacers, and his dam Justissima, while getting her record on the trot, had a gait very suggestive of her wanting to pace, and part of her foals did pace. I can remember at least one that was a pretty fair pacer. I predicted that the stallion Adios, 1:57½, when he was old enough would make a good sire, and I believe the results bear me out. One of his dams appearing in his pedigree was Lady Maud C., 2:00½.

Some day trainers will elect to use as much skill and patience in training and balancing their pacers as they do their trotters. When we do we will have a great many pacers that will look almost as nice as some of our trotters. Too often the trainer listens to the advice of bystanders and caretakers, who always advise hopples. I never put hopples on any of La Paloma's colts during their yearling form.

There was a time when Lexington would not permit a hopple pacer to start. Smart Ben Walker told this one: The mare Little Squaw had always raced in hopples. He was invited to drive her at Lexington. In those days horses wore breechings as a part of their harness. He let hers down about where hopples would strike her behind so that she would think she was wearing hopples. He won a betting race with her.

Once I had a pretty bright fellow say to me, "What you want to balance him for—he wears hopples? Just iron him off." To be sure hopples are a very necessary part of our training equipment and there will always be horses that will really need them to race in.

In order to encourage the racing of horses without hopples, how would it be to offer a bonus to drivers winning with pacers which did not wear hopples? It might be all right to offer a few races barring hopples, but for a time at least it would draw a light entry as it did in the past.

I do believe, however, that nearly all pacing colts should be trained in hopples until they have, at least, reached the 2:30 stage in their training. It will help the gait and manner them better, and if it has been decided to put hopples on them later, they will know what they are. The old argument that once they are used to hopples they must always use them hardly holds water. How about Sep Palin taking the hopples off of His Majesty and beating two minutes with him? Fred Swaim took the hopples off of Abbe Scott when she had a record of around 2:14, and won races with her and went in 2:02½. Very few pacers that race without hopples seem to need shadow rolls. Billy Direct did not wear hopples and many of his get race without them. I am told Delvin Miller is using some wise ideas about hopples. "Though the mills of God grind slowly, yet they grind exceeding small." At best, it will take a long time to mold public opinion to make careful selective breeding, and a long time to change the opinions of most of our drivers about hopples. Had it not been so hard to buy hopples when Jimmy Highland and Captain

The World's Champion Greyhound, 1:55¼, with Sep Palin up.

Pointer began their training, they would have worn them; and I doubt very much if they would have raced as well.

Lately I have been thinking a great deal about stallion supports. The runners do not use them and I noticed the late Dr. Parshall trained many of his younger stud colts without them. I have noticed that most stallions draw their testicles up when in motion. Stallions like Joe Patchen II and others with large testicles and weak cords probably need them.

Dr. C. G. Schwindler, V.S., has now passed on. I raced Captain Pointer, 2:02½, for him. He and I were good friends.

A race that I was rather proud of was the Free-for-All Trot at Muncie, Indiana. I drove the horse Donald A. and won the last two heats, beating a really good field of trotters. The heats were 2:08½, 2:08, 2:07½ and 2:08, and were really the world's record for four heats over a half-mile track for a time. There were John Gallagher, 2:04½, Coasta J., a very good half-mile track trotter, Christy Mac, Ellie Trabue, and as I remember it, three or four others. Anyhow, it was the best field of trotters to come together over an Indiana half-mile track. It was my first and only time to drive Donald A., as he was in Gabe Cartnal's stable and Gabe could not be there to drive him. That same week I also won a good race with Captain Huertus, beating a good pacing mare that had been winning right along.

How the memories come—memories of the happy days and months and years—thirty-seven years—I have spent at the Indianapolis State Fair Grounds! I made friends with many wonderful people. The trainers with whom I associated were among the top ones. There was Sep Palin, who had raced many great horses and had to his credit the world's fastest trotter, Greyhound, 1:55¼. One of his most outstanding patrons was Colonel E. J. Baker, who owned

Greyhound and many other exceptional horses. Another patron was Castleton Farm which races so many unusual horses. You can add to this a horde of owners of good horses which Palin drove, among them Her Ladyship, 1:56¾, the world's champion pacing mare. When he passed on the world lost a great horseman.

Then there is Homer Walton, who likewise has accomplished much. He was the first trainer of Her Ladyship, also of Frisco Dale, 2:00, Green Valley 2:00, and many horses with lesser reputations. One of his principal owners is Charles Jackson of Chicago, a wonderful fellow. He owned Her Ladyship and His Majesty and he owns a pacer now that looks to be of two-minute calibre, and races nearly all the time over the half-mile tracks. He is a nice horse and bred as I like them bred. He was sired by Chief Abbedale, dam by Colonel Armstrong, a good son of Walter Direct.

Homer was in the cavalry in World War I. He spent many nights rolled up in a blanket, sleeping on the ground. He told me that he made a vow that if he got back to the States safely, he would never make a kick, no matter what happened. The way he has lived up to that pledge makes all of us admire him. As further proof of the man's exceptional courage was his reaction to the loss of his eye. I was in the accident which caused that loss. The colt I was driving made a break in front of his colt. His colt tore my right wheel down, but I was able to ride the sulky to the outside and pull up. One or two others were involved in the accident, which broke the leg of one man. In the mix-up Homer's eye was gouged by a sulky shaft. Although it was a racing accident and unavoidable, I have always been saddened by the terrible thing it did to him. In his love for his chosen profession, however, he drove races afterwards. Handicapped by the loss of his eye he handles horses in big fields, which stamps him as game as they come.

And I think of others—of Charles McGown who races horses well and whose work with Peaceful Abbey was outstanding; of Dennis Shell, who has raced a lot of good horses; of Jake Mahoney, who had a lot of excellent horses to his credit; of Fred Swaim, now with the runners, who used to do splendidly with the harness kind. We all loved and admired Frank Tracy for his personality, and brother, how he could drive a horse race! Charles Hammons, who has passed on, could race horses well and had a knack of dealing them off. He could sell horses when none of the rest of us could. Indeed, he had a great deal of ability.

Charley used to tell these stories about Dan Burge, an old driver who had reached his peak and was on his way down about the time I started.

In one of them Dan and another driver finished in a very close heat with a pair of rough hopping-gaited trotters. The judges, not sure of themselves, decided to call both men to the stand and get their versions. With his quick Irish wit Dan said, "Well, gintlemen, it was a hop-skipping race and I out-hopped him."

Another was in the good old days when there used to be somebody close to the fair grounds who would run a boarding house the week of the fair. In those days they did not figure so closely. On this occasion there was a big plate of fried chicken on the table when the men sat down. A husky young fellow next to Dan started to take a nice piece of the chicken when Dan said, "Hold on a minute, young man. We ginerally say a little something before we eat here." Embarrassed the other waited and then old Dan, saying "Go!" speared the piece of chicken.

I am not sure whether it was Charley or Clay Hasch who told this one. Dan's home town seemed to be Dayton, Ohio. Anyhow, somebody from over there let Dan talk him into sending a colt south with him for winter training. About every week the owner would get a glowing letter about the colt from Dan. The owner had provided a nice new outfit for his colt. A week or two passed without him hearing from Dan and one day he thought he saw him walking along the street. Hurrying, he caught up with the man and it was Dan. After the usual greetings the owner asked Dan about the colt. "Do you know, that colt died," said Dan. After the shock had worn off a little, the owner asked, "Well, what did you do with the cart and harness?" Replied Dan, "I thought so much of the colt I just buried the outfit with him."

There were many others, too, no longer among the living, who were outstanding in the world of trainers and drivers. There was Mart Wilson who had the facility of getting horses going good and then getting them sold well. How many times I have laughed at his witty stories! Horsemen used to take him with them down to the Old Glory Sale in New York just for the sake of his enjoyable companionship.

Then there was George King, who was a great trainer and expert at balancing his horses. Alex Wishart stood out as a colt trainer. Clate Dagler was very successful. He trained horses a lot for Abiram Boyd, who was a remarkable breeder and owner. He bred La Paloma and several others that distinguished themselves. His Hazelridge Farm was an important place and Mr. Boyd knew how to drive a horse himself. He is still living, and what pleasure we have talking over old times!

Again there was Dick Wilson—not a brother of Mart Wilson, but a relative—considered one of our very tops as a race driver. He won the M. & M., a great trotting stake at that time with the gray horse John Taylor. His friends still talk about the brilliant drive he gave him. Bumps, a pacing gelded brother to Moko, one of our great sires, he gave a record of 2:03¼ several years ago. He raced many great horses.

Then I think of J. B. Chandler, known in his day as an outstanding trainer of colts. He was quite a wit. I remember I was jogging beside him one day and I said, "Mr. Chandler, your colt has his tongue over the bit" Quick as a flash he replied: "Well, it's his tongue." He won the Kentucky Futurity with Peter Sterling and brought out the stallion Bingen Silk, a fast three-year-old and a good sire.

There was Millard Sanders, who brought out the great Lou Dillon, 1:58½, our first two-minute trotter. He had many other exceptional horses and was unusually skilled at developing speed. And one remembers Ed Allen, who did a lot with the great Single G., but who also raced many fast horses and was noted as a driver. His twin brother Hammie was also good, especially with a trotter.

Too, there was Bob Wright, who trained the Montour Farm horses not far from Pittsburgh. He used to winter at Indianapolis. He was a fine fellow and trained many excellent horses. Harrie Jones, Harry Snyder, Ed Lewis and Billy Hasch are all gone, but I remember them with admiration.

Another very great horseman and trainer was John Benyon, who was at one time second trainer for Mr. Geers and later for Mr. Murphy. His brother Ed raced successfully down the Grand Circuit for years. His son Jimmy gave Argot Hal his record of 2:07¼ on a trot. I greatly admired Argot Hal. He came from the great Hal pacing family. He was a handsome stallion and appears to be one of our outstanding pacing sires.

And speaking of families, John E. Madden says in his book, *Life With the Trotter,* that the family is greater than the individual. Sometimes we find a horse from a wonderful family that doesn't amount to much as an individual, yet because of his inheritance other horses descended from him or her may be very remarkable.

It has been my observation that usually in the ancestry of any great horse we will find somewhere on the maternal side a great mare.

Among us today is Jimmy Wingfield, now one of our tops and liked by everybody. Also there are Mr. Midbo, Ty Drook, Don Taylor, George Sholty, Walter Dispanette, Everett and Thomas Eads, Riley Walters and his son Muriel, Clay Hasch, George Keys, and Harry Beatty, who could develop such extreme brush in his horses. His son Wilbur is among the best of the younger reinsmen of today. And I cannot forget William Maple, who owned, managed, and gave much of the training to Walter Cochato, one of our notable Indiana pacing stallions. Many of his get raced well.

Many horsemen remember Reece Howe, whose trucks hauled the horses around to the race tracks, to sales, etc. Reece worked for Ed Lewis for years, toward the last driving some of his horses. We all liked him. His last years were devoted to the trucking business. He has passed on, but we feel his life was shortened by an auto accident that left him badly crippled.

A certain veterinarian, also deceased, was another whom we all liked. I always considered him one of the very best of diagnosticians. I remember one case in point. I owned a half interest in a colt which had gone lame. We could not find the trouble and had to turn him out. One day I took Doc out to see him. After his examination he said, "Well, Clair, you cannot see anything now, but you will find he will show up with a ringbone some day." That is exactly what happened and we sold the colt to go on the scrap heap.

The new owner fired the ringbone and he finally ended up with a trotting record of 2:10¼ over a half-mile track.

Doc always liked the runners and had a hop receipt that was a good one. Before the U. S. T. A. came into being and before the sputum test was used to detect drugs administered, it was a common thing for those in charge to hop a horse and not much was done about it. These things are funny to me now. I was racing at Crawfordsville and it was easier to drive home each evening than to stay there. A competitor in the next day's trot said to me, "Clair, I wish you would stop there at Doc's and bring me a bottle of medicine." "Certainly, Denny," I replied. The next morning when I stopped at Doc's, as he handed me the bottle, he said, "Better watch out. He will beat you this afternoon. This is a bottle of hop." Well, my competitor and I had the two best trotters by two or three seconds. Added to that he had drawn the pole. I reasoned that if it was left to brush he might beat me. When the word was given we left trotting like a pole team and we trotted that way to the seven-eighths pole where his horse, hop and all, gave it up. He made a break the next heat and I won easily.

Along the same line I have laughed often about another incident. Here in Indianapolis at the State Fair after the owner of a mare that was to race had gone into the grandstand, the driver called Doc in and, waiting until the caretaker had gone after a bucket of water, he had Doc give her the hop medicine. She won that afternoon, her ears set forward, looking for a bigger town. I was the only witness and Doc and the driver knew I would never tell. I had brought the mare out and generally raced her. The owner and I were good friends and how many times he has happily told me about that great race his mare had paced. They have all passed on now and though I have laughed about it many times, this is the first I have told it.

After the U. S. T. A. came into being, a friend of Doc who was high up in the horse world got him the job of paddock vet at Lexington. I used to chuckle when I would think about him being in there giving sputum tests when he was one of the most expert in the country hopping a horse. Doc was really a good fellow and smart.

Needless to say there are many others whom I have not named who meant just as much to me. I like to think I am one of the Indianapolis training colony. I have valued their friendship, their advice and their companionship down through the years a great deal more than they ever suspected. Many times I have incorporated ideas from some of them about rigging, training, or balancing a horse in my stable. Among the newer trainers whom I do not know so well but who seem to know what it is all about are Carl Quinn and Gene Sears.

The horseshoers who have shod horses for me here at Indianapolis are very able and I have long enjoyed their friendship. In addition to Clarence Cole are Hood Elder, Jack Ball, Buzz Lee and Denny Lee. Buzz and Denny Lee's father, Art Lee, used to shoe for me also. When out to the races I have had shoers from all over the country, and what a big part they play in the success or failure of our horses! One can't be too careful to remain in the good graces of these hard-working, skillful men. The wisecracks and the kidding I have received in shoeing shops would make good copy for any comic magazine writer. Maybe I have kidded them some, too.

What a lot of wonderful men love the harness horses! Some are owners, some used to be owners, and many come around just because they like them but feel they cannot afford them. I have seen veritable giants in the business world sitting contentedly on a bale of hay, talking to a very ordinary man about the merits of some colt they owned.

Yet that same listener would have a difficult time, indeed, were he to try to get past a bevy of office girls to talk to such business men. Whether the owner owes a sizable sum on his home or owns a railroad makes little difference to the real horse lover. It is his attitude in which the horse lover is interested. Does he love horses? Will he do what he says he will do? Will he take defeat like a gentleman and be sport enough, when his horse goes a disappointing race, to be glad his opponent won?

Along this line they tell a story about Mr. Dickerman, who owned the fast mare Nedda. For some reason she had gone a bad race that day. At the close of the day, he rose, remarking, "Well, I must go down and cheer Harry Fleming up. He will feel miserable after her showing today."

The owner has made the money to finance his horse, but he should remember that the trainer rides long miles jogging him, often in very inclement weather, too. It is the trainer who spends hours thinking how to rig and balance him, who tries again and again to find out the weight and kind of shoe best suited to him, who determines just where he goes best with his overcheck, and countless other things. Of course, he is paid, for he has to live just as everybody does; but no owner can begin to pay for the happiness and satisfaction the trainer feels when the horse makes good.

I love to think of the many wonderful men who owned horses I have trained over the years and also the many I have met who were owners for other trainers. Such men were often in the business world, quick-thinking, up on their toes, yet if you bring them to a stock farm or a race track they will shed all that and become happy over the showing of their horses. I have seen an owner miss going to a big city to look after an important business deal, yet attend an auction of trotters to buy or sell a colt. Loving horses seems to bring out a side that would otherwise be unsuspected. He will become humble, patient, and just naturally a "good feller."

An owner of whose friendship I am proud is Otis Anderson of my former home town of Lafayette, Indiana. He has bred and raced some good horses. Dennis Shell first and then Clay Hasch raced his horses successfully. To mention a few: Brown Prince, 2:00, Battle Prince, 2:00, Cardinal Leeds, 2:01⅘ trotting, and Atomic Might, 2:02⅗, which paced in two minutes separately timed.

One fall at our fair August Born had the trotter Single Spud, 2:02½, in our stable. I had known his father many years before and therefore felt very near to Augie, as we all call him. Through him Mrs. Wolverton and I came to know his wife and two children and his mother, and the following year his brother George. Later George bought a colt and trained him a season or two. The Borns are a wonderful family to know and have for friends. Augie has a lot of natural ability as a driver. Single Spud is a fine trotter. It so happened that the horse I was racing went lame and we put the groom I had on Single Spud and took him over and trained and managed him. Augie would only come and drive him on race day. That fall we took him to Lexington and Augie gave him a breeder's record around 2:07 and later in the week started him in a race where he made a splendid showing. He could not go away fast but could finish flying. The next two seasons he got so he could get on his stride and go away fast. While his record is 2:02⅗, I feel sure there have been times when he was capable of trotting in two minutes. His dam being by Single G., one could see many of the old warrior's mannerisms and looks about him. I enjoyed training and being around Single Spud. My last sickness made me lose track of him, but I feel certain that unavoidable things kept another good trotter out of a record of better than two minutes.

There is still another class of men who are, indeed, very necessary to the success of our horses. I refer to the caretakers. They come from all walks of life and for various reasons. Many have spent their more rugged years in some other work or business and in the twilight of life have turned to the race tracks to care for the trotters. They soon become fascinated with the sport and all its many angles and end up by being expert at looking after horses. In doing this work that they are still able to do, they can make the most of a life that otherwise would be boring. Many of our top trainers of today began their careers by thus taking care of horses.

I have spent many hours in the company of caretakers laughing at their jokes and wisecracks. Sometimes when the day is over and they have had a few drinks—occasionally one will, in their own vernacular, get "his tongue over the bit"—and just the right kind of audience is present, perfect gems of wit and philosophy will drop from their lips. Drivers, were they within earshot, would often get a shock to their ego when a group of caretakers discuss their ability in a sulky. Years ago, sitting in the barn office one winter afternoon and listening to a caretaker telling of the mistakes of a certain trainer's handling of a particular horse, I said, "Well, just what method would you use if you were training that horse?" It caught him off guard and I have often wished that my fellow trainers could have listened to his prescription.

It is of their devotion to the horses of which I like to think most, however. How many times I have seen a caretaker, while his horse was still eating and before he, himself, had gone to breakfast, stoop, remove the cotton and run his hand over one of his charge's legs that was a little "suspicious"! How many times have I seen them standing at the stall door after the horse has raced that day, watching him eat, making another trip in to straighten his blanket, to feel his body to determine if it was just the right temperature and if he has cooled out just right!

Years ago there was a caretaker with the nickname of "Mike, the Tramp." And could he take care of a horse! However, he seldom stayed long on a job. Under no condition would he rub a pacer that wore hopples. One fall he picked on a pacer and for some reason he stayed all winter, a record for Mike. A short time before the racing season started, the trainer decided to use hopples on the horse for which Mike was caring. That afternoon and evening Mike tidied up the horse's trunk, washed all his bandages and blankets. An old head said, "That's a sure sign. Just watch. Mike is going to take a 'run-out powder.'" Sure enough, the next morning Mike was gone before the trainer arrived. Money due him made no difference in his decision to run out. Sometimes, months later he might see the owner and collect and sometimes he wouldn't even try to collect.

In times gone by what a host of nicknames they had! I can think of Hickory, Fine and Dandy Slim, Hump McCoy, Brandy, Box-car Riley, Jimmy Few Clothes, Hard Roads Jimmy, Dyspepsia, Tom Easy-Goin', Roarin' Bill, Surething Jimmy, Fatty Sheets, Red Farr, Shadow Roll Frank, High Ball Whitey, Salty, and Guppy. Some derived their nicknames from some horse they rubbed, such as Spill, Sweet Marie Bob, etc.

What expert judges of human nature many of them are! Somehow they seem to have the knack of saying the right thing. I have found another way to have some fun is to get unnoticed near a walking ring and listen to the kidding the grooms will give one another about the way their horses raced that afternoon. Colored grooms will say things that are sidesplitting.

Many an owner or trainer has sat in his hotel at night, happy over the way his horse raced that day and knowing full well the groom is doing everything possible to make the horse comfortable.

I used to get a lot of kick out of Box-car Riley. He seemed to follow a pattern. After the last races in the fall he would go to Dallas, Texas, and winter with another old head. We used to say that spring had come when he appeared at Lafayette. He would come into my stable and, without a word, start cleaning a set of harness, and he would have a stock of stories and happenings to relate as only he could tell them. One day at Fort Wayne someone sent him to the stable after a sulky whip. As he passed me, he said, "I wonder what that laundryman did with my colors?" He came from a responsible family and they were always glad when he would show up. On this occasion I think it was Hickory who was with him. Anyhow, while they were washing up for supper Riley said to him, "I suppose I will have a car fit when I get in that bed tonight."

Many an old-time trainer whose children have grown up and married and whose wife, perhaps, has passed on, finds himself alone. He can go back to taking care of horses in surroundings with which he is familiar and be happy with people he knows and understands.

The years they spend around race tracks make many grooms pretty fair judges of a prospective trotter or pacer. Life's vagaries, its denials and disappointments, may have spelled the difference between a man being a groom or the owner with his attendant responsibilities.

Chapter VI

COLTS AND STALLIONS

O N A TRIP to Lexington not long ago I attended the trots, visited stock farms and sales, met old friends and made new ones. It was a pleasure to meet Jesse Shuff again, whose weekly column in *The Harness Horse* with Lexington horse news I always enjoy. It was delightful to talk with him of horses and horsemen we had both known in other years.

What impressed me particularly, however, was that the University of Kentucky was giving a course in stud management which included lectures by veterinarians on the breeding season. It occurred to me—for the subject is very near my heart—why should there not be lectures and leaflets available for people who are breaking in our fine colts to drive? Owners very often pay thousands of dollars for a colt or filly, then turn it over to a man who may be both a crack trainer and driver, but is not very interested in the breaking process and who may even pass the job on to a groom. If he does it himself it is quite possible that he has not broken many colts in his career and that he will use the methods of someone he has observed.

Thus I think men like Hunter Moody could doubtless give lectures or get up a paper of their own theories and methods of breaking colts. By making these theories and methods available, not only would the novice be helped, but even those more experienced might profit, especially if ideas could be exchanged. In that way stock farms with light training carts could employ some man skilled in breaking colts in their weanling and early yearling forms.

Colts never forget their breaking lessons. They become still easier to handle and less apt to hurt themselves. Perhaps they will drive a little green for a day or two when they begin their fall training, but with the breaking lessons over they are ready to begin the fall and winter jogging and training. Many owners and trainers would appreciate this and many a colt would escape improper methods of breaking. Sellers would find this would pay off in the long run.

Over the years I have seen colts get some pretty rough breaking lessons. I remember one case a long time ago of a nervous, high-keyed mare, perhaps a four-year-old, which was subjected to trip ropes and tin cans tied to her tail. She would kick viciously. She had a great deal more intelligence than the men who were breaking her. She finally got so she could be driven in 2:25 and became a nice-gaited trotter. Who knows, however, if she might not have trotted a great deal faster had she been differently handled? Her breaking experience made her quite a dangerous mare around the stable. She was started a few times under the name of Carrie Nation and believe me, she was every bit as much of a fighter as was her hatchet-carrying namesake.

Once in Indianapolis I was passing the fair ground and while I was not close enough to see who it was, I did see a colt hitched to a cart. The colt had thrown itself and was getting a lacing from the whip of the trainer while three or four big helpers stood near. After a while such a colt will catch on to what is wanted and, probably with repetition, get to driving satisfactorily. And I presume that colt breaker will tell what a tough one he was to break. Was he or was he not the victim of misapplied methods?

Just as with children and grown-ups who do not want to fit into our pattern and who make for themselves and for us plenty of trouble, so it is with our horses. Some of them, as a last resort, do have to have harsh treatment.

In our kindergartens and schools we have trained personnel. Wouldn't we as parents and grandparents be up in arms if our children were not carefully treated and trained? Then why shouldn't our brainy, highly-bred colts be broken with as much proficiency and patience as we use with our children?

Before the starting gate was used many a colt, under the excitement of his first race, would show some of his improper breaking lessons, generally the turning left or right in turning to score. Educators have found that children cannot keep their attention on any one thing but a short while. I have had colts break out in a sweat the first few times they are harnessed and turned loose in a stall. The harness made them nervous, of course.

I have had colts come in to be broken and the first day I would leave them in the barn to get used to their new surroundings. If they had been broken to lead I would put a halter on them and lead them out and around the place they would see when they got their breaking lessons. How many times I have heard men say, "He's gentle. He won't do anything." True, he had been handled by men ever since he was following his dam, but that doesn't tell you anything. He shouldn't be afraid of men, but he has still to learn the first lessons he will need before he competes in races. The colt that throws itself and gets all twisted up in its harness and cart, are we sure it is not hysterical rather than mean? Maybe it is confused and doesn't know how to proceed with its lesson and maybe the lesson is too long. It probably does not and never will know why it is being whipped.

We are told, and I believe it, that a horse has only a single-track mind. Should we not be careful then to teach but one thing at a time and add to our teaching as the colt's progress warrants? In the past I have seen men line driving colts, using an open bridle with a long pair of webb lines and no guy rope on them. The colt goes along watching its driver, is stopped and started even before it has thoroughly learned to go forward. This is all good, but it can be done still better. For these first few drivings I like a driveway barn and use a blind bridle and have a guy rope attached, so that if he gets tangled up in the lines you can still stop him with the rope. If that fails you can still catch him if the doors are closed. The next best is to drive him up and back along a fence. As with children, make his first lessons very short, possibly five minutes, then turn him into his stall with the harness on and let him get his bearings. You can go and jog another horse or go down to the blacksmith shop for the relaxation of a little conversation and some good laughs. Then come back, take your colt out now and you will be surprised how much he has improved even in that little time. Give him a couple of more lessons that afternoon and the next few days will please you with the results.

Most people don't like to walk and thoroughly line-break a colt before it is hitched, but if the methods I have mentioned were observed, there would be fewer bewildered colts which throw themselves, perhaps break a cart, and get a whipping they likely will never understand.

I realize there are quite a number of different systems and smart people using them. We tend to cling to those we have found efficacious. For years I broke a large percent of the colts trained at the Lafayette Fair Grounds. Also at

Indianapolis I broke a large number. The last was a few years ago, when in the course of three years I broke a total of forty-nine yearlings while training and letting down older horses. Of course I was ably assisted by the help jogging the other horses. Of all those colts only one got down and that was because his feet slipped on snowy ground. I used one cheap whip which was still good when all my breaking was over and which was either lost or stolen.

Even with all these precautions taken there will still be unforeseen things happen, but in the final analysis the over-all results will be better and many a colt will miss getting wrong impressions.

Many years ago we were required to city-break colts intended for use as road horses. A fellow brought in a nice big three-year-old filly for me to city-break so she could take the place of his old driving mare. Well, I was getting along fine and after a time I invited the owner to get on the break cart with me and ride downtown so he could note her progress. We drove by street cars, different kinds of delivery wagons, etc., and through narrow streets. Her deportment was perfect. I was about ready to turn her back to him. I had an open bridle on her and about a half mile from the fair ground on the return trip, I invited him to raise an umbrella which I noticed he was carrying. Well, it frightened that filly and did she give me a time for a while! He sat up there like a dummy, apparently never thinking to lower his umbrella. I learned from that that it isn't wise to overplay your hand. It was all my fault, for he would never have thought of raising that umbrella in the first place if I hadn't suggested it. He was the kind of man who fit Billy Marvin's laughing description of a good solid citizen with money in the bank, who wore his hat a certain way and generally carried an umbrella.

I am a great believer in using a hemp guy rope in a colt's

mouth until he is quite well along with his breaking lessons. Your colt will have a hair-trigger mouth and will be more apt to obey a pull on the lines if it is necessary. His lips will get a little sore, which you want so he will obey the reins more readily, but they will heal almost immediately when the rope is discontinued.

Years ago a friend of mine was breaking a colt, which was acting nicely and he had never been obliged to restrain him with the lines. One day something frightened the colt and my friend was pretty busy getting him stopped. He had to resort to a Springstein bit, which is severe, and even with that he would try to run for quite a while afterwards. I am not too sure that some of our side-reining horses are not the result of someone having to take a severe hold on them and bruising one of the gums in front of the bit teeth. I can think of another fellow who knows his way around who doesn't believe in using a rope in a colt's mouth, but uses a roping halter instead. Thus opinions differ.

On a trip to Lexington I was brought up with a start when I saw all those two-minute miles by our colts today. Whereas we used to speak proudly of 2:05 records, we will now speak of 2:00.

How often I have thrilled at a field of two-year-olds marching by the grandstand in perfect alignment on their way up to the starting gate! A fifth of a second may spell the difference between first and second money. We have bred them for this sport and they like it. Let us keep them free of unpleasant memories.

I may be old-fashioned, but I still like a pole cart that will carry a helper with a guy rope on a colt. Have a good-headed horse to hitch the colt with and drive him a few times on the off and near side. Before you hitch him single, drive him a few minutes with the lines without any cart. Ninety-eight times out of a hundred the colt will give little trouble. You will save yourself a great deal of walking, the colt will like the companionship and take his cue from the older horse, which will help in teaching him to turn right and left. Always avoid turning the colt sharply. He will learn it himself as he gets more experience.

In bitting colts I like to have the back strap plenty long and buckle the girth very loosely. I use sash cord for the overcheck and check him loosely. Also the side lines should be slack and I even buckle a small strap under his chin in the rings of his bit to keep the annoyed colt from pulling the bit through his mouth. These can all be tightened gradually as the colt gets used to them. Moreover, I like to lead the colt around before I attempt to line drive him. One will be surprised how nice a colt can be if properly bitted.

I used to know a family of colts sired by a hard-to-manage little old son of Axtell. Almost without exception they would throw themselves, breaking back straps, girths, overchecks, cart shafts, etc. When I saw one of them I would almost bet it was sired by that horse. Maybe some of it could have been avoided the way colts are handled now.

I like to break and even train a colt in a blind bridle for quite a while before I put an open bridle on him. Whenever possible I use an open bridle in racing and to quiet very high-keyed horses in training.

When the colt is ready for his first driving lessons to a cart I like to line-drive him, and then equip him with a breast collar, take the traces in one hand and the lines in the other, let him take a step or two forward, then put a moderate pull on the traces for a short distance. This will help a little to give him the right impression when he starts to draw a cart. When the colt is hitched the first time or two he will be bewildered and want to stop to get his bearings. Have your helper, who should be leading him, stop and give him a few reassuring pats on the neck and after a moment or two start forward again. How many times have I driven a colt out one door, along the barn and in the other door, unhitched him, turned him into his stall for thirty minutes or more and then hitched him again! When the time is ripe have your helper ease back from the colt's head and walk beside the cart. Drive him a little farther if you are getting along well. Unharness him now and then, and later hitch him a couple of times more. Do this for a day or two and after that you will be well on your way. After your colt gets a little confidence very likely he will pull a fast one which the driver will have to deal with as he sees fit. Always keep in mind that your colt learns by repetition and that those first lessons are very important to him.

It is my hope that the U.S.T.A. will endorse a procedure for colt-breaking, taken from those whom they think qualified, and make such procedure available to colt buyers. Many a colt would thus escape experiences he would be better off without and it could be your high-priced colt, Mr. Owner. I still think stock farms would be doing a great thing for the colts and for the buyer if they would drive a colt ten or fifteen times.

And now we come to the subject of stallions. Once their racing and training days are over, it is pleasant to think of our older fillies and mares in the fields with their foals, enjoying themselves as nature intended they should. Too, once their racing days are over, the geldings are often turned into the field with the mares, or are agreeably employed one way or another.

But one can't help but think of the stallions once their racing days are over. Some of them are finally put on stock farms, where their attractive breeding, individuality, and racing ability make them desirable to use in the stud. If these stallions could talk they might tell you that their days spent in a training and racing stable gave them the most happiness and contentment. There they have the companionship of other horses on the track, on the walking ring, in the busy training stable, and in the shipping truck. They get enough exercise to keep them healthy and free from being bored.

One of the most distasteful experiences and the most dreaded by our prisoners in penal institutions is solitary confinement. Very often a stallion will be getting a little unsound or be getting into a hard class to win money. For sentimental reasons his owner may not want to sell him, but retires him away from the racing grind to what he considers a reward for his race-track achievements. But is it? Very often he sends him up to his farm which may not be entirely equipped for a stock farm. Perhaps the man in charge is not very interested in the horses and has many other tasks to do besides taking care of the horses. Therefore, the stallion may be placed in a good box stall with plenty of feed and water given him two or three times a day. He is not in training and very often there is no suitable place to exercise him and no men who are not already too busy with other work. Therefore, we find the stallion standing in his stall day after day, the busy attendant feeling it unsafe to leave his top door open when he is not around.

When we think about it the situation is much like Edgar Bergen's keeping Charley McCarthy in a suitcase between shows. Some stallions through isolation, boredom, and lack of exercise finally get cross and dangerous. We find people who are unsocial and disagreeable to be around and we naturally shun them. And in the same way some stallions become downright dangerous to handle. But a large percentage are that way because of the boredom and isolation of their lives in retirement.

The wild horses are presided over by a stallion taking over a band of mares.

Many years ago a physician friend from Ohio used to tell about the stallion Highwood, 2:21½, at one time a good sire. In the later years of his life the doctor used to turn him into the pasture with the mares. He said that many a time he had gone out to the field and caught him and handled him with just a halter. Maybe the exercise, freedom, and the companionship of the mares had much to do with his being so tractable.

The Crouches from Lafayette used to import draft and coach stallions. They said they had often purchased a stallion out of a team and generally hitched with a mare. About this same time our own stallion Dick Red accidentally got out of his stall at the fair ground. We had five or six of his weanlings running around the grounds. While I did not see it myself, the grooms told me it was more than an hour before they could catch him and that he seemed to be having the time of his life playing around with those colts.

Where farms are not provided with race tracks and training facilities, it is an easy thing to break most of these stallions to ride. Then when the sons or daughters visit the farm they can, with a little caution, enjoy riding them about the farm and in safe places. Thus the stallion will get needed exercise roaming around the farm and be freed from boredom. Appreciation and admiration may be built up in the young people and in later years they may sponsor a race horse. Horsemen very often had relatives or they may have had other contacts which decided them to sponsor harness horses when opportunity offered.

I am of the opinion that the staleness we observe at times in our horses is almost never caused by too much training but rather by the excitement of racing.

Therefore, Mr. Owner, if you want to reward that stallion which gave you so much pleasure at the race track, try to do so with exercise and the companionship of other horses in close proximity.

Chapter VII

LATER YEARS

ONE day at the close of World War II when I had gone back to training horses, Mr. Lake came into my stable. I had known him years before when we had both been young men and lived at Lafayette. I had almost forgotten him. Well, anyhow he made arrangements with me to train a trotter he had acquired, and thus an owner started who is now a very prominent owner of Grand Circuit horses. "Tall oaks from little acorns grow." That mare did not train good enough for a trotter. In the meantime he had bought Jimmy Highland, then a colt, and also his dam from a widow whose husband had always liked the harness horses.

In our talks that summer Mr. Lake and I decided to attend the trots and the sale and try to buy a colt. We visited Walnut Hall Farm the week before the sale, looked at the colts and marked several fillies to bid on, hoping that some would be within our price range.

Come sale day and he was called home for a day or two, leaving me to carry on. I remember that I bid on the mare Ahead Again but did not get her. She later got a record around 2:04. My next try was on the filly Coming Out and I landed this time. My selection was based on Jeanette Rankin, 2:03¼, a really high-class Grand Circuit trotter,

Jimmy Highland, 2:02¼.

appearing close in her pedigree. In addition to her pedigree, Coming Out was quite a nice filly.

I had trained a little mare for Dr. Cotton up in Indiana. His son Alan, who gets around, said to me, "When you go to Lexington this fall I will introduce you to a friend who might really go places as an owner." The very next morning at the race track at Walnut Hall Farm, I happened to talk to Mr. K. D. Owen again, who was the man Alan meant. Mr. Owen said to me, "I tried to get your attention last night. I was going to have you go on if you liked her." We talked a while and he let me know he would buy a Volomite if I saw one we liked. And was I pleased and happy! After all these years I was to have a chance to train horses that I had personally selected. That night Mr. Owen, Alan, and I attended the sale. My selection was Laurelite and a few minutes later, at Alan's suggestion, Scotch Melody was added. Thus in two nights a Grand Circuit stable was born with owners who had both the money and nerve to go big time. We took the two Volomite fillies and Coming Out back to Indianapolis and broke them. Mr. Lake brought in Jimmy Highland to be broken, and he also acquired Shiloh. I was permitted to name her after the famous battle in the Civil War. I had selected her after training her a little, but mainly because of her breeding. She was sired by Frisco Dale, 2:00, her dam by a very fast but unfortunate son of Empire Direct, 2:07¼, the dam of which was Bessie Bonehill, 2:05½, which was also the dam of the great Joe Patchen II, 2:03¼. Empire Direct sired many Indiana pacers and was a great deal faster than his record if he had been sound. I have forgotten the name of the dam of Shiloh, 2:10, but she had a half-mile track record around 2:11¼. She was owned and trained by Jesse Palmer, one of my good friends. Jesse used to tell me that she once paced a mile in 2:04. She produced several that could go around

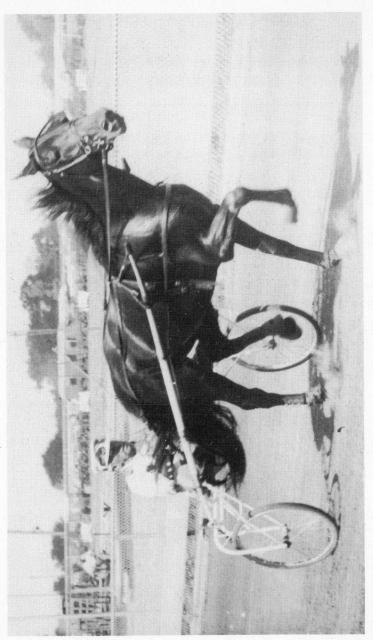

Laurelite, 2:03¾, with the author up.

2:08. The next dam, if I remember correctly, was by Anderson Wilkes and was the dam of Harvey K., 2:04. Shiloh got a record over a half-mile track of 2:10, but I recall timing her in 2:04 in a race. She may not produce a colt pacer, but I have a feeling that a really good aged pacer will some day be descended from her line.

My first trip to Southern training grounds for winter training was at Macon, Georgia. Just before shipping, Captain Pointer, a coming three-year-old which later got a record of 2:02½, was added to the stable. He was owned by another of my good friends, Dr. C. G. Schwindler.

I enjoyed the winter, and in addition to being with my old friends Mr. and Mrs. Ora Dunkin and Ky Trowbridge, I made many new ones. Leon Toole, I discovered, could really drive a trotter. Phil Stuart shod most of the horses, and what a nice fellow he is! Among others I grew to know and like were Mr. and Mrs. Burch and Mr. Jones, both local owners and patrons of Ora Dunkin and Leon Toole. Then there were Mr. and Mrs. Stanley Tweedie, Johnny Dill, Herb Roth, Robert Plexico, Mr. Craig, and a few others.

Our first start was at the Toledo Meeting. Laurelite started right out to be the good consistent race mare she always was. She was second there in a stake for two-year-old trotters and trotted in 2:09½. Captain Pointer won his race.

We shipped from there to Goshen to the Historic Meeting, a place that I had always hoped I could visit sometime. I have forgotten, but as I remember it the horses raced pretty good. We shipped some of the horses to Saratoga, where Laurelite trotted well up in the money in a stake. Frank Woodland, whom I had known as a young fellow, was speed secretary. I also met Ted Gibbons, who qualifies as a square shooter and in my estimation is a very nice

Her Ladyship, 1:56¾, winning at Syracuse with Carty Nagle, 2:00, at the rail finishing third. In the next two heats the daughter and son of La Paloma finished one, two.

person. Ted's father used to train horses, among them Palestrina, 2:09½, which is the dam of Dean Hanover, 1:58½. I saw a picture of her in Ted's rooms.

From Saratoga we took some of the horses to Roosevelt Raceway, where Walter Gibbons held forth. I knew Walter a little better than I knew Ted. I have a great deal of confidence in both men and they are the kind who will do to bet on. The horses raced pretty well there. We raced at Good Time Meeting at Goshen and on through to Lexington. Captain Pointer won at Du Quoin and at Lexington, where we sold him. Laurelite always raced well and Jimmy Highland kept coming on and racing satisfactorily. Coming Out kept us thinking she was a good mare, but she was always getting lame one place or another.

We finally had to let Scotch Melody go to pacing and she came flying right after we came back from Lexington. She worked a mile in 2:09½ free-legged. I have since thought that had she been raced free-legged, she might have raced to a very fast record and then might have trotted as some of them do.

At the sales that fall Mr. Owen added several more colts to our stable. It was decided to place Scotch Melody in other hands, and they raced her in hopples. While she got a record of 2:04½, I noticed she got so she would stutter a little going away, probably because of the hopples.

Mr. Lake added Record Express and Miss Morris Chief to our stable and we wintered at Aiken, South Carolina, a really delightful place to winter-train horses. I got to see a great deal of Mr. and Mrs. Frank Ervin and Mr. and Mrs. Harry Whitney, all of whom are considered tops in the training and racing profession today. Frank Ervin, in addition to his natural horsemanship, is an extremely hard worker and has forged his way to the very peak in his line. His phenomenal success with the biggest money winner,

Record Express, 2:04, raced by the author before he was injured at Springfield, Illinois.

Good Time, should be glory enough, but not for Frank. Among the best he handled were Adios, 1:57½, Scotland's Comet, 2:00, The Colonel's Lady, Yankee Hanover, The Tippler and Sampson Hanover. Frank's father, too, was a great horseman in his day and raced among others the horse Riley B. with a record of 2:05¼.

I used to like to watch Harry Whitney train his horses. He seems to have a knack with a trotter and drives a smart horse race. His success with Chris Spencer was outstanding, to say nothing about the other good horses he drove. He had a wonderful owner back of him, Mr. Dunbar Bostwick, who owns the track at Aiken, stands very high in the affairs of the U. S. T. A. and drives his own horses in some of their races for the sheer pleasure of it. He drives with skill, too.

Billy Haughton was just getting nicely started that year and is now one of our most competent drivers.

That was the same year that Laurelite, Coming Out, and Jimmy Highland were three-year-olds. Jimmy Highland was coming in to a nice pacer. I won with him at Saratoga and was offered a good price for him. He raced well all season. I was very high on Coming Out. The week previous to the Historic Track Meeting she had worked around 2:12, coming the last half in 1:02. I felt she was getting good. But come race day and she suddenly became very lame at the start of her second warming-up heat, making it necessary to draw her. There followed several weeks of rest and treatment, but not until we shipped her to Milwaukee and Harry McKay injected a muscle along her spine with his famous medicine did we get results. The long lay-up, however, had made her lose form. Harry Whitney drove her her first race following the Historic Meeting. She raced well for him, and followed by being second in a stake for Clay Hasch at Carthage. At Lexington Frank Ervin drove her and we timed her close to 2:05. This was to be her last race as she went lame again coming on to the track the next spring for a slow workout. A nice-gaited trotter with inherited racing instincts, why did fate step in and deny her reaching the high form of which she appeared capable? Surely a high-class trotter will descend from her some day.

I loved to drive Laurelite because of her racing instinct and dependability, and also because Mr. Owen had allowed me to select her. Mabel Trask, a very great trotter appearing on her maternal side, had a great deal to do with that selection. A racing accident at Springfield, Illinois, broke my collar bone and kept me from driving for a few weeks. The other drivers were wonderful to me and drove my horses whenever they did not have one in the same race. I had recovered enough to drive her at Lexington and was second with her in the Kentucky Futurity. She trotted a brilliant race and I was a very happy man that night. I did not know it then, but this was to be the last race of any consequence I would ever get to drive.

I had the pleasure of seeing Mr. Owen refuse a nice price for Laurelite from Gianni Gambi, the Italian buyer who is a good judge of a trotter. She is retired now and I enjoy visiting at Walnut Hall pastures and just looking at her. She is my idea of type for a brood mare and perhaps that dream trotter will be descended from her.

Royal Comet was another of my selections. He was hard to train at first, but got to racing satisfactorily. It was my fault for not realizing it, but I have a feeling that his testicles kept him from becoming a high-class trotter.

I was very high on Penelope Hanover, a nicely bred, good-gaited trotter. I got to drive her only in her first race where she was well up to Mr. Derby's good roan filly driven by Frank Ervin. Thereafter fate stepped in with minor sicknesses and mishaps of one kind or another, keeping her from reaching high form. In the end nobody believed in her much but me.

Serious illness overtook me at the Harrisburg Sale, rendering me unfit to drive races any more. Though I trained a little and managed the stable, Stan Stucker was engaged to do the race driving. He is a young man with a lot of skill and good judgment and is not afraid. He has a good chance to go far in this business.

We opened at St. Louis and started off with a bang. Laurelite trotted a heat in 2:04 and came a last half in 58½ seconds. Jimmy Highland and Record Express both raced well. We shipped to Historic Meeting at Goshen where Record Express trotted a sizzler, winning the first heat in 2:07 and being beaten back a whisker in 2:05 and 2:05½. She was a good trotter and had a right to be. Her dam was the great producer, Lookaway Express, and Record Express was sired by one of the good sons of Volomite. I timed her on several occasions that summer close to 2:03.

We went to Old Orchard, Maine, where Jimmy Highland won in 2:04. Laurelite was barely beaten in 2:04, and Royal Comet was right there. Then at the Good Time Meeting at Goshen we thought we had a chance in the Hambletonian with Record Express, but a racing accident spoiled it. As I remember, however, the others raced good. Also at Springfield they raced well. At Sedalia Jimmy Highland was really remarkable, going to the front early. He paced handily in 2:02½ and Miss Morris Chief was timed separately in the same race in 2:04. Before that at Lexington we had won a stake with her either as a two-year-old or a three-year-old in 2:07¼—I don't remember which. But going back to the Sedalia race, we timed Laurelite a mile in a little better than 2:02. Royal Comet trotted better than 2:07 and was up close. Record Express also did well.

Coming back to Du Quoin, Jimmy Highland won again.

He got to be a nice pacer and still is. The other horses, too, were right in there pitching. Finally we wound up at Lexington. Royal Comet won a race over the wet track and the others raced satisfactorily. Penelope Hanover got a breeder's record around only 2:11¼, but I timed her in a race one day in 2:07½. I am told her first foal, as a nice two-year-old pacer, could go around 2:02. I believe they call him The Tippler.

Mr. Lake and Mr. Owen were wonderful to me, backing my judgment in the selection of their first horses. We went big time and did not do badly either. Owing to my health it was only wise for them to place their horses in other hands. Harry Fitzpatrick and Frank Ervin are now handling their horses and have brought them to new successes. Other high-class horses have been added. Any good fortune that comes to either Mr. Lake or Mr. Owen gives me pleasure.

The mention of Springfield in connection with the stable brought back to mind another of my friends, Henry Hawkins, now retired. Illinois can be justly proud of him. He was very skillful with a horse on a race track. In years past when I have raced in Springfield sometimes I with others have been a guest in his home. He was a delightful host and we would all laugh heartily over the clever way he had of relating funny incidents. One of his stories in particular I have enjoyed telling. However, he told of one incident which was touching. In a near-by field were several mares, one of them blind. Two or three times a day one of the others would maneuver her up to the big watering trough for her to get a drink. I like to think about that. There will always be plenty of room in this business for the Henry Hawkins kind.

Omer Amunsden and Foy Funderburk were two others with much ability and also fine men to know.

Early one morning in Lexington, while I was still in charge of the Owen and Lake horses, I happened to sit down at the same breakfast table with Mr. J. C. Simpson of Pittsburgh. As horsemen are sure to do, we soon fell to talking about our beloved sport. A little later Mrs. Wolverton and I met Mrs. Simpson and we feel we have added new friends to our list. Mr. Simpson later introduced me to Mr. Brown, a friend of his, whom I very much admire. The Simpsons and Mr. Brown are the kind of people who mean much to the sport. The last year I was in charge of the Lake and Owen horses, while we were at St. Louis we got to know still better Mr. and Mrs. Fenner Hawkins. We occupied adjoining motel rooms and Fenner and I used to drive out to the track together. I soon saw that he really knew a lot about his subject. He was a crack judge of a prospect and could race and train with the best of them. He was still with Mr. Blake. Dell Cameron was doing the race driving. He called my attention to an older member of the stable, Brittanic. What a good horse he was! Fenner had selected him after he had gone through a series of little mishaps, just enough to discourage the other owner. He had an eagerness to do his driver's bidding, with a sharp brush. I grew to be one of his fans. He raced against Laurelite several times that summer; and while I wanted her to win, if she was to be beaten somehow there was less sting when Brittanic did it. That summer, while he was warming up for a race at Springfield, he dropped dead. I was so deeply touched I could not refrain from writing about it. Mr. Blake cut it out of *The Harness Horse* paper, made a beautiful framed copy of it and sent it to me. It is now hanging in my home. I am appending the tribute, hoping it may please some horse lovers:

"Brave Brittanic, what an example to cringing men your glorious passing!

"Warming up for the game you loved so well, in your devotion to duty and desire to do your driver's bidding, you disregarded death's summons only to fall crashing through her very door. Gamely rising to your feet you fell again. It was as you, brave horse, would have wished it.

"They say you are buried at the seven-eighths pole, your head placed toward the finish line. This is the place that you with your beautiful gait were wont to start your electrical dash that spelled defeat to many a trotter. A lettered stone to mark your last resting place! But you, dear horse, have a far more beautiful monument in the hearts of those who knew and loved you.

"If there is a heaven for horses, and we hope there is, what a gala day when your brave spirit returned to its keeper.

"We all loved and admired you, 'Britt.' "

Mr. Blake stands very high in the affairs of the harness horse, and his stable is one of the very best. Dell Cameron gets to drive those wonderful horses and what a fine showing he is making! His brother Dana has charge of another good stable and he also is a very excellent driver.

I like to think back on my visits to Goshen's Historic Meeting where Mr. Al Saunders for the last several years has played important roles in two. As has been said, Goshen and the surrounding country is "the cradle of the trotting horse." I remember my visits to the monument of Hambletonian 10, hallowed ground to those who love the horse who was the fountainhead of the trotter; to the Charles Backman farm where the great stallion Electioneer 125 was foaled and sold to Senator Leland Stanford where he was put at the head of one of the two most important breeding farms of that era, Palo Alto. Mr. Charles Marvin was his head trainer and his accomplishments with the wonderful colts produced there made history. He wrote a book in which he set forth some rather unique training methods insisted upon by Senator Stanford. The Senator also indulged some of his theories on the effect of thoroughbred blood in the trotter. The most notable of his horses was Palo Alto, 2:08¾, a great trotter of that era, the dam of which was a thoroughbred. The Senator used to set a row of cameras to study the gait of his colts. Who knows but that may have been a beginning towards the motion picture industry!

I visited the farm where the great Goldsmith Maid, 2:14, received some of her early training and where the outstanding stallion Volunteer 55 is buried.

When one goes to the Historic Meeting and is greeted by dear little Mary Stuart he is put at once at ease. Then when you look around you discover that nearly every man, woman, and child is trotting-horse-minded. In fact, I noticed a group of children in the charge of a lady, perhaps their teacher, enjoying immensely the horses both in the stables and on the track. Those who come to the races from Goshen and the country around it are a genteel, well-bred lot who really know and love the trotter.

I was greatly impressed by Mr. E. Roland Harriman's business sagacity and influence in the founding of the U. S. T. A. by a horsemen's meeting at Indianapolis. He was, of course, ably assisted by other men of brains and prestige, yet it would seem to me that his unselfish devotion to the best interests of this great sport is worthy of some special demonstration by the horsemen. His position in the financial world is such that our gifts would be superfluous. Mr. Wiswall attended that meeting and played an important part in its formation. Before it is too late, why could not the horsemen give a dinner in Mr. Harriman's honor and have Mr. Wiswall, who is a gifted speaker, appraise him of our gratitude? And we are grateful. During the years

St. Roch, 1:59½, (C. Dean).

when this sport was dependent upon the National and American trotting associations for its rules, it almost owed its very life to Mr. Harriman. Indeed, it might be likened to a newly-born foal on unsteady legs, which under his supervision has become a wonderful flashing trotter of which none of us are able to predict the finish.

Mr. Harriman's trophy presentations and his eulogy to the memory of William Dickerson—Billy Dick as we all so fondly called him—are beautiful to think of. Mrs. Harriman is a very accomplished horsewoman. I remember seeing her drive Tassel Hanover a fast mile in public. A former caretaker told of having to get busy and clean up some horses that they had thrown out of training before Mr. Harriman's mother came to see the horses. I like to think her interest in the trotter may have passed on to her son and caused the great interest he has shown in the harness kind.

Any success that comes to the Arden Homestead Stable or to Harry Pownall is welcome news to me. Two local ladies, Elizabeth Rorty and Frances H. Wallace, would surprise you with the knowledge they have of rigging and training horses.

Very likely the greatest single contribution to harness racing was Steve Philips' starting gate. It was his own original idea and probably I saw his very first tryout at North Randall. It has solved many of the problems that confronted a starter under the old system. We old-timers can readily appreciate what it has done for the sport.

Two men who have played a very important role in the harness horse interests in Michigan are Jim and Andy Adams. Andy has owned at least two first-class trotters. At the time of which I speak they had Tommy Winn, one of Michigan's foremost trainers, driving their horses. Tommy got hurt at Hillsdale, their home town, and I drove their

trotter Arion Guy Scott, winning in 2:06½, and beating a
good horse driven by Chase Dean, that had won a string of
victories up to that time. He was a game little horse that
was not beaten until the judge said so. Again Tommy could
not be at Franklin, Indiana, so I drove Arion Guy Scott
another winning race, beating a good mare.

Arundel Stout was another good trotter owned by Andy
Adams. W. N. Milloy raced him and if memory serves me
right he won at Lexington in 2:02¼. Mr. Milloy raced several good trotters in his time and was a true gentleman.
Brad Compton is racing their horses now very ably. He first
raced the horse Earl Junior, winning with him as a three-
year-old at Peoria in 2:10¼ without hopples and beating
two of our Lafayette horses. He was then sold to Walter
Cox, who put hopples on him and raced him for years. He
got to be a good little grey horse. Brad has raced many
good horses for the Adamses as well as for others.

Jim owned the fine trotter Hi-Lo's Count, selling him to
Leo McNamara. Hi-Lo's Count did not stay sound for Leo
and he is letting Brad and Jim try him over again. He is a
very fast horse and I am keeping my fingers crossed. Jim
and Andy have raced a lot of horses and have an extensive
knowledge of harness horses.

Going back to Chase Dean—he first raced Sir Roch,
1:59½, before George Loomis got him. He also raced
Summer Song, 2:06½, owned by the same man who had
Sir Roch. That man was, I am sure, Mr. L. O. Randall of
Chicago. Also Chase raced horses for Walter Cox for a time
and did well with them. I can't remember them by name,
but down through the years he has raced many good horses.
It was Townsend Ackerman who raced the horses before
Chase got them—the ones that he raced at Hillsdale. Townsend could do much with a trotter and was a very prominent trainer down East.

This brings to mind little Charles Mabrey. The things he accomplished with horses were legion. He was a product of Madison, Indiana, and when just a boy the first horse he raced was Rand, 2:18½, with which he did big things in a big way down in Indiana. He came to Indianapolis a few years later and raced for Fred Cline, who eventually got to be a prominent owner. While with Mr. Cline he raced the trotter Choir Boy, a grey horse, giving him a record of 2:10½. He won a sparkling race at Lebanon, Indiana, with American Belle, 2:12½, a free-legged pacing mare, and beat a horse called Dick O'Donnel, 2:08½, an outstanding young pacer at that time. Charles Mabrey then went down East where he was very colorful. He drove Widow Grattan, winning at least a heat and keeping Grattan Bars pretty busy to beat her in a $25,000 race. With a trotter called Subpoena he won a $10,000 race. Another sparkling race to his credit was at Lexington with a trotter in 2:01½. Charley was small of stature and on that occasion Townsend Ackerman picked him up and waved him around as if he had been a little boy. He won a lively race with Chief Abbedale over Cold Cash. He was high on Chief Abbedale and predicted he would make a good pacing sire.

Ben Walker was at the height of his career about the time I began driving races. Then and for several years afterwards, he was considered the greatest catch driver of his day. He appeared to have a knack of being able to drive any strange trotter or pacer. In the sulky he seemed absolutely fearless and some of his mounts certainly didn't have Sunday School manners. Late in life, after his race-driving days were over, he used to go down the Grand Circuit sometimes, tending the gate at the grandstand enclosure or holding the flag when the flag was used. The last time I remember seeing him was at the State Fair in Indianapolis. I recall he held the flag the day Hal Dale got

Billy Direct sets the World's Harness Horse Record at Lexington, Ky., in 1:55, driven by Vic Fleming.

his record of 2:02¼. Hal came the last quarter in 32½ seconds and actually shied as if he was playing as he passed Ben at the flag stand. I will always think he could have paced that mile in 2:00.

Ben was quite a bit older than I, but I enjoyed him immensely, and I remember I had him over to the house for dinner during our fair. The high-class horses he had driven down the Grand Circuit and his accumulated wisdom made him a delightful companion. I believe he at one time drove the horses of "King Maker" as Monroe Salisbury was called years ago. If Ben is still living he is in California, since he seemed to have a liking for the Golden State. He could really drive a race horse.

All you have to say is "Vic" on any race track and horsemen will instantly know you are talking about Vic Fleming. He still holds the world's pacing record of 1:55 with Billy Direct. I saw this and was I proud! He also holds the world's double-gaited record, 1:59½ and 2:00 with the mare Calumet Evelyn. Everybody was excited over the Billy Direct mile, especially Vic's son William. Vic was a truly great race driver and his success was wonderful. He once told me that if you have a horse that would stop a little, to keep right on racing him, if possible over the ice in Canada. He said your horse would race better and go farther the next year. He called my attention to a horse then in his stable. A deplorable accident had ruined his health enough to put him on the side lines.

Everybody admires Vic. His sons, William, Charley, and Jimmy, are all top notch race drivers. William has driven several races for me and did them well, too. Like their father, they are wonderful to be around.

The Gahagans are a very important part of this business. Joe was a Grand Circuit driver, who spent much of his life around Toledo. He raced a grey trotter, Doctor Strong,

2:05¼, down the Raging Grand and did well, too. Like all of his family, he was a wonderful person. I can't remember his other horses, but he numbered among his patrons J. J. Mooney, a very high-class owner. The other three were turf scribes. George has spent many years in Indianapolis where he was identified with *The Western Horseman*. He also had an interest in the Central Publishing Company. I always rated him right along with Joe Markey, who was really tops. Tom reports the G. C. races ably and has done it for a number of years. Will was, for a time, on *The Chicago Horseman,* then he came back to Indianapolis and worked on *The Horseman and Fair World*. He went from there to Goshen where, under Mr. Harriman, he took charge of the Trotting Register. He remained until his death. He left a talented family, all of them with a flair for writing. His daughter Agnes, now in charge of the Museum of Trotters at Goshen, was the announcer at their race meeting, and what a nice showing she made!

Any Gahagan is an asset to the harness-horse business. I thought I was expressing my admiration a bit by naming a colt I had bred Gahagan. For a time it looked as if my good intentions had backfired. The colt, in some of his stall antics, lamed himself before I had him fairly broken. We could not feel certain we had found the trouble that season or the next until later we fired him. Dr. Bishop, who hails from Canada but is associated with Hagyard & Hagyard, remembered the colt and bought him. It takes a good pacer to go in 2:10 in the part of Canada he is in. As I have mentioned before, in Nova Scotia Mr. Adams used to tell me the air slowed up a horse about three seconds. Gahagan made good with a bang and I am happy about it now.

I had a very high regard for Fred Terry, who owned *The Horseman and Fair World,* and passed it on to his son Robert, who not only carried on with the paper, but sponsored some of our important stakes. One of them is our leading stake for two-year-old pacers, the Fox Stake. Fred and his son have both proven wonderful over the years.

Fred had a very interesting early life. For a time he and his father handled and sold standard-bred horses on the latter's farm. They sometimes mated them up in fine teams and all in all handled a great many horses. Fred showed me how to attach a guy rope to a colt you are breaking that is, I believe, by far the best method I have ever seen. It looks a bit foolish to me for a man to line drive and break a colt in the early stages without a guy rope attached. He really should have an extra man along for a time.

Fred bought and shipped a lot of western horses to the St. Louis market and got caught in the panic of 1895. He then worked for a time on *The Chicago Horseman* and finally came to Indianapolis to work on *The Western Horseman,* owned by Dr. Neal of Charleston, Illinois. Later Fred bought the paper.

Another driver with outstanding ability in his day was Vance Nuckols, a son-in-law of Al Pennock. Mr. Pennock drove a lot in this country and then went abroad. He exported the futurity winner, Siliko, which was in "Knap" McCarthy's stable, a big event in Knap's long life with the trotters. An accident in a race caused The Abbe, driven by Ben White, to be distanced after he had won a heat. Knap was replaced behind Siliko with "the wonderful man from Freeport," as M. E. McHenry was fondly called, who went on to win. Siliko was bred and owned by the outstanding John E. Madden. They used to tell of Knap that when he would come in from driving some colt he would say, "Just like Siliko."

Mr. Pennock returned to this country after a few years, bringing with him the trotter Willy. The last time I re-

Peter Astra, 2:01½, with Doc Parshall at the reins.

member seeing Mr. Pennock he was racing secretary at the North Randall Meeting. He was a fine man.

And speaking of North Randall, a touching thing happened there. Single G. had made his final appearance in a race before the Clevelanders, who so much admired the great horse. Age had finally overtaken him and Harry Devereux, whom we all admired and loved, made a farewell speech and presented a beautiful blanket as a token from North Randall. There was many a tear in the eyes of old-timers.

While I was still a young man, Charley Hayes and H. B. Sheppard gave many of the later Grand Circuit meetings at Columbus. They purchased the pacer Independence Boy and raced him until he finally ended up in the fast class with a record of 2:01½. As I have mentioned, this horse probably had a lot to do with Charley A. Valentine's rise as a prominent driver.

I got to see a lot of Charley Hayes in the next few years while racing around Ohio. I liked him. His son Christy, who was about my age, Benny Sturgeon, Ed Keller, and I were usually companions to the track and back again to Toledo. I really enjoyed those weeks and the others in the Ohio short ship. Since those days Mr. Keller has forged steadily ahead. Christy was much like his father and one enjoyed being around him. He drove a pretty good mare, belonging to his father and himself, in those days. He still owns horses, among them the mare Filly Direct.

During these years I have never seen anybody like Benny Sturgeon. He could drive any kind of horse well and seemed to know what to do in any situation. He always had plenty of catch mounts. Wherever he was he was the center of entertainment. I was always a ready audience and I think he really liked to make me laugh.

Chestertown, 2:00¾, with Tom Berry up.

Dick McMahon had been in a serious race-track accident which left him with a crooked ankle and wrist. Benny used to get around the draw gate where Dick was and imitate him. It would have been offensive if anybody else had done it, but even Dick would laugh at Benny. He and I were warming up horses at North Randall and he would tell regular sidesplitting incidents just to hear me laugh. He has passed on and I miss him. Those were good old days to think about.

Doc Parshall, now deceased, and to whom the great Thomas W. Murphy presented his colors when he himself retired, was also a wonderful horseman. For a few years he won a great many races while he was at the peak of his profession. His selection of Dudley Hanover, while he was a trainer for the Hayes Fair Acres Farm, was outstanding. His early training of that horse may have had much to do with the splendid things he later did. I believe Dudley Hanover will be a great sire also, as a truly remarkable mare figures in his dam's pedigree. Doc, too, brought the great Pronto Don out. In all, the notable things he did and the famous horses he brought out were legion. There were three brothers, all of them beating two minutes. Kings' Counsel, Chief Counsel and Blackstone were only a few of the many renowned horses he raced.

The Hayes Fair Acres Farm has raced good horses for a number of years, but in these last few they have really done things. Dudley Hanover and Pronto Don are two illustrious horses, to say nothing of several other horses which have raced with distinction. Benny Schue, as head trainer, and Fitzpatrick have driven these horses with extraordinary skill these last few years.

Keen little Mrs. Winings, as I have mentioned before, spotted a great driver when she first called my attention

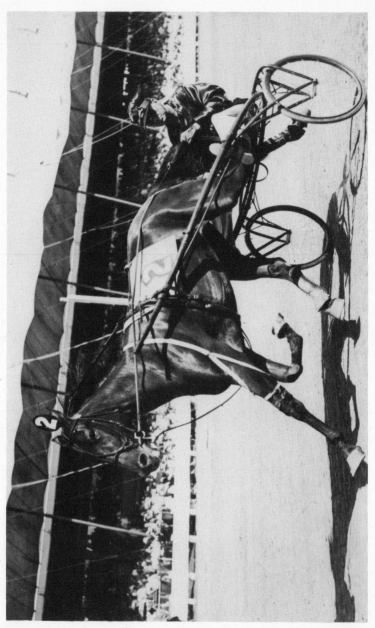

Miss Tilly 3, 2:01⅖.

to Tommy Berry. I have been watching him ever since and I am agreed with her. If he had done nothing else but race all those famous horses for the Hanover Farm, including winning the Hambletonian and Kentucky Futurity with Hanover Bertha, it would have marked him as unusual, but on through all these years he has accomplished many other things. He wound up the season in 1953 winning the Kentucky Futurity again, this time with the colt Kimberly Kid 3, 2:00½, 4, 1:59.

I am also an admirer of Fred Egan. Like Tommy Berry his career has been a distinguished one. He won the Hambletonian at least twice. He has had many good patrons and his late sponsor, Mr. C. H. Phellis, qualifies in my book. Fred won the Hambletonian for him with Spencer Scott and Miss Tilly and developed for him that remarkable colt Hoot Mon, which he sold to Sep Palin for Castleton Farm. Sep won the Hambletonian with him.

Mr. Gage Ellis with the Village Farm, and the sires Abbedale, His Majesty, Royal Napoleon 2:00½, Follow Up and others, played a very important part in the breeding interests. Gage's sponsoring of the Abbedale Stakes, as well as other prominent positions he has held, mean much to this sport.

Walnut Hall Farm, first started by L. V. Harkness and managed by Harry Burgoyne, has come on down through the management of Mr. and Mrs. Edwards and is now two important farms. The Walnut Hall is operated by Mr. and Mrs. Nichols; the Walnut Hall Stud by Mr. and Mrs. Sherman Jenney. They have kept abreast of the times from the very beginning, constantly incorporating the strains of blood which produce winners. The number of great horses produced there over a long period is amazing. In the past I have bought many colts there for different owners and some have distinguished themselves.

When Mr. and Mrs. Hawkins were at Walnut Hall Stud, Mrs. Wolverton and I visited there often and came to feel we were well acquainted with Mr. and Mrs. Jenney also. Lawrence Brown has been the capable manager of Walnut Hall Farm for a very long time. His friendship and advice are valuable.

I remember I saw the colt Fire Glow led there at Walnut Hall Farm before he was sent to the New York Sale. I was very impressed with him even then and but for his untimely death at three, he might have been one of our very best trotters.

Castleton Farm, too, operates in a big way and the high-class horses they can and will produce can scarcely be estimated. They can hardly miss with such an exceptional band of brood mares and headed by several of our very great racing stallions. Mr. McKinzie is the manager of the horse department at the farm. He is an Indiana product, coming from near home and believe me, any one of those McKinzie boys will do to bet on.

I am, of course, very proud of the Two Gaits Farm not far from my home. Mr. Mac, as we call him, has accomplished much. He is very prominent in the affairs of the U.S.T.A. and has always helped with our I.T.P.A. When he represents his farm at the sales, he is the best I have ever seen. I could not help but notice how he had the confidence of important buyers. He has constantly weeded out and added to his band of brood mares until now they compare favorably with those on any farm. His stallions are second to none. His judgment in the selection of mares and his knowledge of those to whom the colts are sold has had much to do with the phenomenal success of Hal Dale as a sire.

Two of Mr. McNamara's sons are taking over the stock farm end of it now and Mr. Mac himself is enjoying the racing stable, which does very well, too. Ralph Baldwin, who is racing the stable, is one of the very best. He seems able to drive any kind of horse creditably. One thing I have noticed—he generally has his horse in a good spot before he tries for a heat.

I am very interested in the doings at Frost Hill owned by Mr. Roy Amos, who is just getting nicely started but has already bred the world's two-year-old champion trotter. His father raced for years and years and won his share, too.

Mr. L. B. Sheppard, who really runs the Hanover Farm, occupies many important positions. The head of the U.S.T.A. has a big stable of horses raced by the Farm. Mr. Sheppard drives a race occasionally and is the Farm representative at the Harrisburg Sale for the largest consignment of colts by any farm. His eleven-year-old daughter drove the great Dean Hanover his famous record mile of 1:58½.

Mr. and Mrs. Rex Larkin of Poplar Hill Farm are making themselves felt in no uncertain terms. They have raced horses very successfully down the Grand Circuit for years and they know their way around. Their first, that I remember, was Ann Vonian, 2:01¼, which was herself a high-class pacing mare. When her racing days were over, one of her foals was Poplar Byrd, 1:59¾, which was not only a good race horse, but a good-looking one as well. They are crossing several Billy Direct mares on him. It looks to be a sure-fire way to breed high-class pacers. We had our mare Allegra in foal to him and felt pretty good about it.

The above-mentioned farms with many smaller ones are all operated by men with brains and vision, and surely it augurs well for the future of the trotter.

Marvin Child is another driver I very much admire. The more money bet, the better he could drive. He would bet his own money, too. He raced many good horses, among them two which I liked especially—Hal Mahone and Hal Bee. I always thought he could do more with the giant trotter Cupid's Albingen than anybody else. Among other horses I can think of was Calumet Adam, 1:59¾, and, of course, there were others with slower records. He now holds a very important position with the Hanover Shoe Farm and is highly regarded in the horse business.

No doubt every horseman has his own ideas and ideals about gait and conformation in the horses he admires. Of the living stallions of the pacing gait, I believe I like best the gaits of Adios and Jimmy Creed, plus their pacing inheritance. Adios is already a top pacing sire, and horsemen will soon wake up to the value of the extreme speed inheritance and gait of Jimmy Creed as a stallion to which to breed mares. Both these stallions, when they raced, could not only go very fast, but their gaits suggested perfection even at top speed. Nearly everybody in the horse business knows and likes Cy Thompson, who owns Jimmy Creed, and who certainly knows his way around.

Cy's father, William Thompson, was also very successful in the horse business. He bred, among others, the stallion Hal Dale, 2:02¼, which, by the way, was another pacing stallion which had my ideal of a pacing gait. Mr. Thompson sold to A. A. McClamrock of Frankfort, Indiana, Hal Dale's dam with Hal Dale still following her, and a grey and a bay mare. The bay mare raced good on the trot for several years and, I believe, ended up with a record better than 2:10 over the half-mile tracks. It also runs in my mind that the grey mare raced creditably. I am also quite sure that Mr. Thompson bred Frisco Dale, 2:00. He bred and trained and raced a number of excellent Indiana horses during his life.

I raced the gelding Prince Direct down the Grand

Circuit one year for Mr. McClamrock. We did not want to give him a record that year, but I do remember we worked him in 2:04 at Lexington. James Hazelton, a great stallioneer, was with Mr. McClamrock for a few years, and I think Walter Direct made his early seasons in the stud at the Frankfort Fair Ground. Another stallion to which I bred the dam of Checkers, 2:06½, was Oratorio, 2:13, and I sold the filly as a yearling for a pretty fair price for those days.

Another prominent Indiana horseman is Pearle Hungerford of Shelbyville. Green Valley, 2:00, and Frisco Dale, 2:00, and later Guinea Gold are among the horses he has raced. His son Paul now does the race driving and does a good job of it.

Shelbyville brings to mind Bert Wallace, who was a very successful trainer and race driver. Everybody who knew him liked him. I was among the witnesses to the tragic racing accident that caused his death. Philip Hill of Bloomington, Indiana, owned several of the really good horses Burt raced. Philip has passed on, but he was a wonderful owner. He bred the mare Abbe Scott, 2:02½, and raced her some. Howard Gordon was another of Bert's patrons, and who, pray tell me, who gets around does not know Howard?

Still another Shelbyville trainer is Fred Johnson, who has been in the game a long time and has raced a large number of horses successfully. And Fred Runyan is another trainer who has made good. Harold Boring is one of the younger ones, but is already achieving. During World War II I trained the Josedale horses in Shelbyville for two seasons and found it a very satisfactory place in which to work.

To me, Colby Turner is one of the most remarkable men whom I have ever seen. I am told that at a very early age he got caught in a corn shredder, severing both arms above the elbows. Despite this handicap he has trained horses and driven races for years. I saw him drive a race and was simply amazed at his skill. How he can hold one together and help a tired one! He fastens the lines together, places them over his shoulders and uses the stumps of his arms to guide and control his horse. If he has a horse as good as yours he is just as apt as anybody else to beat you. His courage and judgment are wonderful. In his home state of Ohio they are so used to him that he attracts little attention, but to me he will always be marvelous. Owing to his age I doubt if he is still driving races.

Mr. Henry Knight of Lexington is another who has done outstanding things in the trotting affairs of this country. I am quite sure he bred and sold our world's champion trotter. He was the first to race the great trotter VanSandt, 2:00½. Primarily he is a big operator with the thoroughbreds, yet his doings with the trotter as a campaigning owner and breeder are notable.

I keep thinking of the extraordinary things Colonel E. J. Baker has done. He has raced famous horses, and the moral support he has given to the trotting horse interests can never be discounted. Owning and racing the world's champion trotter Greyhound would be glory enough, but add Winnipeg, 1:57½, Cardinal Prince, 1:58½, Algiers, 1:58⅘, His Majesty, 1:59½, and a horde of other remarkable horses he has raced and one wishes that the years on earth of such a man could be doubled. Let us not forget, however, that Sep Palin was responsible for much of his success. Neither can one help but think that Mrs. Van Lennep, in riding Greyhound under saddle to the world's record, was influenced to establish the famous Castleton Farm, the early success of which was in part due to Sep.

Harry Fitzpatrick, who gave Algiers his record, is one

of our outstanding trainers of today. The high-class horses he has raced, the races he has won, and the important owners who have patronized him speak volumes. His son Jimmy seems to have inherited much of his father's ability. Indeed, he is bred to be a good horseman from both parents, his mother being the daughter of Walter Dunn, a man I much admired. Walter owned a stock farm near the Charleston, Illinois, Fair Grounds. He had a stallion, Argot Wilkes, 2:14¼, which, I am told, was a very fast horse, at the head of his farm. He sired a lot of speed for those days and he was considered game. Walter trained and drove most of his own horses; and although he is a rather rugged man, I saw a horse he called Si Plunkard go two miles with him the wrong way of the track in spite of all he could do. It brought again to my mind that you can't hold a horse with a pair of lines if he really decides to go.

Alfalfa, 2:05, sired by Argot Wilkes, was a very high-class pacing filly and raced for several years successfully for John Pender of Johnstown, Pennsylvania. Pender often drove Alfalfa himself and how he liked to talk about her! He was a smart fellow around a race track and would bet large sums at times. He liked the way Ben Whitehead drove a horse and both men were hard to beat when the money was down.

I always thought Ben Whitehead could take a horse to the front early in a mile, save him, set the pace and drive him more skilfully than any man I ever saw. Ben brought the stallion Etawah, 2:03, out, selling early that season to Mr. Jones, who was Mr. Geers' patron. "The Grand Old Man" won the Kentucky Futurity that fall with him. He was one of the best gaited trotters I have ever seen.

One cannot help but pay tribute to Ben White. His sterling character plus unusual ability has rewarded him

with many triumphs over a long period down the Grand
Circuit. He won the Hambletonian four times. His first
win of that greatest of all stakes for trotters was with
Mary Reynolds, belonging to W. N. Reynolds, who has
owned many famous horses down through the years. Who
does not know of Mr. Reynolds' importance in the tobacco
world!

Ben's winning again with his son Gibson's filly Rosalind,
1:56¾, now the world's champion trotting mare, was a
popular win to all of us.

Ambassador was the 1942 winner of the Hambletonian
and Volo Song won in 1943. Both were owned by William
Strang, who, at different times, owned several high-class
trotters. He was a long-time patron of Ben. He sold Volo
Song to Colonel E. J. Baker. A few weeks later in a
race Volo Song injured himself so severely he had to be
destroyed. Ben is reputed to have considered him the one
horse which could have lowered Greyhound's record.

But going back to Gibson White: His trips year after
year down the Grand Circuit with his illustrious father,
whose friends and admirers were legion, drew much attention to Gib, as we all call him. Were it not for his inherited common sense, certainly he would have been
spoiled. He has a natural love for the horses and extraordinary ability in his own right in driving.

And Gib has courage, too. At the Grand Circuit Meeting at Duquoin, Illinois, he was well up to the front in a
big field. As he headed into the back stretch, one of his
lines broke near the bit. He climbed from the sulky seat
on to the horse's back, reached down to the bit and guided
the horse safely to the outside, thus avoiding what could
have been a nasty wreck. His nerve and cool-headedness
made quite a hit with Mrs. Wolverton and me, who are
among his fans.

Frank Foster and his son, who own and operate the Houghton Sulky Company of Marion, Ohio, are patrons of Ben and have owned some good horses. Ben always trained and raced Dick Reynolds, 1:59¼, first giving him a two-year-old record of 2:05½ on a trot. He then put him to pacing. He raced free-legged and could go fast and far.

And speaking of Kentucky Futurities, how well I remember the year James Magowan of Mt. Sterling, Kentucky, started the colt Mainleaf by Mainsheet in it! Dick Curtis drove him and he won the first two heats. I will always believe he would have won the third one and the race, but for the fact that while going down the back stretch one of the tires on his sulky burst and he pulled the sulky on a flat. At that he lost only by a narrow margin. It really was a beautiful race. The colored people from around Mt. Sterling and Lexington kept up an almost constant cheering, and, indeed, most of us whites wanted the gallant little trotter to win.

Mr. Magowan also owned the stallion J. Malcolm Forbes, 2:08, that was sired by Bingen and out of the dam of the wonder sire, Peter The Great, 2:07¼. Jimmy once told me he had timed J. Malcolm Forbes an eighth in 12¼ seconds. What a wonderful lot of colt speed he sired!

How surprised I was early one morning during the Kentucky Futurity to hear the then popular song, *Alexander's Ragtime Band*, sung beautifully by a little colored boy, who quickly shambled away when I approached!

Doc McMillen of London, Ohio, is a driver who has been a power over many years. He still stands right at the top of the winning race drivers. I remember him winning the $25,000 trot years ago with Peter Cowl, 2:02½.

Another Ohio driver who ranks high is Gabe Cartnal, who, like Doc McMillen, has won a great many races and driven a number of outstanding horses. Jakey O'Connor was a good pacer for him many years ago. Ohio people loved Jakey. Unless you have a better horse than Gabe, you can't beat him. His son Ken is very successful with the California horses. He has driven several races for me and I like his methods.

This brings to mind an owner in Ohio who was in a class by himself. His name was Frank Callahan, a resident of Tiffin. He generally had one or two pretty good horses. Nearly anybody in the Middle West could tell of some of his wisecracks and sayings. Callie, as we called him, had raced his horses through the Bay State Circuit this particular year and had been beaten quite regularly. As it sometimes happens, he had never drawn the pole at any time. The secretary at the last meeting was settling up with him and said "Mr. Callahan, we will be glad to have you with us again next season." Callie's reply came like a flash: "Yes, when you get ready to auction that pole position off this winter, let me know and I will come down and bid on it."

During the years I knew him he had some of the very best drivers at one time or another driving his horses. There were Ed Abrams, Charles Valentine, Fred Egan, Bob Plaxico, Gabe Cartnall, Vic Fleming, and Doc Mc-Millen, and probably others. His horses generally won their share of the races and he knew his way around on a race track. Some of his more outstanding horses which I can remember were Callie Direct, Fine Girl and Callie G. I was at the Springfield, Illinois, State Fair, had won a heat and lost one in the three-year-old trot with a little horse called Quick Quaker. I was warming him up again a little early the next day when someone far up in the grandstand yelled; "Indiana against the world!" It was Callie.

Mr. Walter Candler is another owner who has played

a big part in the welfare of this fascinating sport. For a long period of years he has owned, bred and raced a number of our great horses. It was he who owned and raced the stallion Abbedale of which Walter Cox once said; "He can go fast farther than any horse I ever knew." It runs in my mind that Mr. Candler bred Abbedale. Fred Egan trained the horses from Mr. Candler's Lullwater Stock Farm for several years and the two men were warm friends. I am quite sure, too, that Nat Ray won the Kalamazoo Derby with a Candler horse. Mr. Candler made a trip to Indianapolis and purchased all of the Peter the Great yearlings at the Fletcher Farm. Included was Elizabeth, the dam of our champion trotter Greyhound. He can drive a horse with much skill himself—in fact, I have seen him drive some of his horses in their stakes. One winter recently at Orlando he drove in the matinees and indulged in training horses nearly every morning. One could not help but notice how lightly the years rest upon him.

Harry Stokes was another driver with unusual ability. Long will be remembered the great races he has driven and the high-class horses he has handled. I was always impressed with his uncommon touch. The horse King Couchman raced perfectly for him. I know, because I was in the same race driving Leila Patchen. King Couchman was then sold for a prospective starter in the C. of C. In other hands he got to be a hard puller. I saw Harry drive him afterwards and there he was, going just as he used to. I am glad his son Donald is coming into his own as a driver.

Billy Andrews was another successful driver of famous horses. I am quite sure he raced the pacer John R. Gentry, 2:00½. It is said that C. J. Hamlin, owner of the Village Farm, paid him the compliment of, "He drives a horse with the skilled hands of a billiard player."

Another notable driver of that period was Mike Mc-Devitt, who raced the horses owned by Mr. Shaw, a prominent Cleveland sportsman. Among them was the trotting mare Grace, 2:04¾, and several other good horses.

A friend of mine who knew Alta McDonald well always told me he was a great horseman. Among those he raced were the pacer Conner, 2:03¼, Dariel, 2:00¼, Sweet Marie, trotting 2:02, and several others.

I feel a little disturbed over the present trend. In the early days some of our prominent owners and breeders would not even train a horse that insisted on pacing. Our meetings then offered many more events for trotters than pacers. Recently I was at Sportsman's Park and noted that the racing card for that night had six paces and two trots. Can it be that the betting public like best to bet on pacers that wear hopples and are less apt to break and "dance on their money?" Let us not forget that our racing associations which sponsor our betting meetings are going to put on the races that encourage the most betting. Let's watch our step. After a time the trotter, which we have spent so much effort in perfecting, can quickly become a hopple pacer; and thus our trotters would be in the same place our pacers used to be. Of course, it won't come quickly, but it could come. We must remember that the public that bets on our harness horses are for the most part people who would bet on the runners, prize fights or anything else. They are not primarily interested in just a nice horse.

Perhaps my vision of splendid free-legged pacers to go along with our beautiful gaited trotters is, after all, only a pipe dream.

On our trip to the Old Orchard Meeting a few years ago we spent the day at the home of Mr. and Mrs. Howard Randall of Harrison, Maine. In years past they have successfully owned and raced several of Maine's very good horses. Mr. Randall has since passed on, but Mrs. Randall is still interested in the sport.

O. P. Munson—"Dink" was the name everybody knew him by—was remarkable in many ways. For one thing he could shoe a horse well. He often shod the trotter Linnworthy, 2:02½. Out at the races he shod a number of horses which I raced in Indiana. Moreover, he could paint and repair sulkies as well as a factory could have done them. In addition, he liked to train and drive the horses and he could drive a race very creditably, too. He had a special knack with trotters, of which he had two really good ones in his last years. He is no longer living, but there will always be plenty of room in the trotting sport for his kind.

It was he who first made me acquainted with Mr. Alexander of Anderson, Indiana, and Mr. Earl and Mr. Thomas Canada of Jamestown, Indiana. I regard their friendship highly. I know the Canadas have never owned horses until the last few years, yet their knowledge of the sport is surprising. The first one they owned was the pacing filly Zoann, which when a two-year-old, I timed carefully at Lexington in 2:04. This one is owned by Thomas. His father has added the filly Miss Ensign, which was just beaten by a whisker not long ago in 2:10 over a slow half-mile track. Both men have common sense, which will carry them far in any field of endeavor. I look for them to go a long way in the future.

Then there is George Byroade, who has spent a great deal of his time at the Indianapolis Fair Grounds and has raced a goodly number of horses. Some of his successful years were spent with Joe Hutsell of Fort Wayne, Indiana. Among the horses he raced which I can remember were Ovelmo Lad, 2:02½, and Gilmartin the Great, 2:09½ trotting, and several good pacers.

Jake Rodman is another who has had many excellent

horses. At one time he drove the Hayes horses, now known as the Hayes Fair Acres Stable. At another time he raced the horses belonging to Mr. Hooper of Murfreesboro, Tennessee. Among these was a pacer to which he gave a record a little faster than two minutes. Also he raced another pacer owned at Cleveland, Ohio. Since going to California he has raced some outstanding horses.

Houston Stone, although a bit younger than either George Byroade or Jake Rodman, has come a long way since he began driving a few years ago. He drove the Hayes Fair Acres horses creditably as well as others I have seen.

A young driver who pleased me the way he drove the filly Zoann was Les Whipkey.

W. B. Taylor was very successful down through the years and his stable was always to be reckoned with, especially in what at that time was the Great Western Circuit. Billy, as he was known by all the Westerners, had his head-quarters for a long time at Sedalia, Missouri. One of his really good trotters long ago was Early Alice, 2:06¼, by Early Reaper, 2:09¾. Billy spent his last years in California and his career ended with a two-minute trotter, Full Bloom, 1:58⅘, which was a member of Gainesway's five two-minute mares.

Jimmy McVey and his brother Howard were successful and their doings in the West were always to be considered. Jimmy did the race driving and one of his successes that I remember was with the mare Minnie Chimes, 2:04¾, a good race mare at that time. He, of course, raced many others which I do not recall. He was a wise little old owl around the race track. One of the last horses which I remember him racing he called Sempro, with a clipped mane. The summer I am thinking of he raced him in Ohio in the Short Ship Circuit. What a thorn he was in my side while I was racing Twinkling Belle, 2:04¾!

Will the many, many horsemen I know whose names are not mentioned here, please understand that they are just as important and stand just as high in my estimation as those about whom I have written. The greatest honor that can come to me is to know and be known by horse lovers, be they caretakers, trainers, owners or track officials. I have been writing this from memory without the aid of year books, Christmas numbers, catalogues, and with only a few horse papers. As I write this some of you have just not come to mind, but you would have been mentioned if you had. Personally, I would rather be a horseman and have the friendship of horsemen than have any other position this glorious country has to offer.

We of this passing generation of horsemen have many accomplishments and happinesses upon which to think back. Every one of you I have mentioned and hundreds I have not mentioned have young admirers, who are hanging on to your very words, your observations, and watching your methods. As you are someone's ideal, you must watch your step.

We have lived with and loved this business a long time. Like everything else that is worth while it has passed through many periods of legislation and has been vastly improved in this new era. All of us can remember when only the stallions and but few of the mares were registered. Many a good horse had breeding untraced after his name. What a great thing compulsory registration is!

Time will gently push us older trainers back and in our places will come younger drivers such as Johnny Simpson, Delvin Miller, William Haughton, Stanley Dancer, Stan Stucker, Jimmy Fitzpatrick, Ken Cartnall, Wendell Wathen, Cobb, and hundreds of others whose names I cannot recall. With smart owners, breeders and track officials there is no telling how far this great sport will go. It is to be hoped that those with selfish interests and bad morals will be kept from getting into key positions.

Many years ago we also had very fast horses, smart owners and drivers. But let us not forget that now we are racing several times the number of horses we then raced, that there are many more standard crosses, that especially the two-year-olds now get a winter and spring training before they race. Add to this the better and more intelligent growing on the part of the breeders, which I believe is not a little responsible for some of the advances made.

Some day the. Grim Reaper on the grey horse will come bearing my life's dismissal. I am hoping to be so busy with the welfare of the trotters that I will be unaware of his approach.

Who is to know but what the spirit world may provide replicas of Lexington, North Randall, Grosse Pointe, Buffalo and other points for horse lovers to go on with? Who is to know but what some of those horses' sportsmanship made them try so hard to win? The only reward they expected of us on earth was food, the companionship and caresses of their owners, trainers and caretakers. I have had horses that looked intelligent enough to talk. Maybe it was just as well they couldn't, for they might have complained about some of the poor drives I gave them.

And maybe these horses which gave owners, trainers, and grooms so much pleasure here below may accompany them to the spirit world. Wouldn't it be a pleasure to go through the spirit draw gate, probably kidding with someone you knew on the knockers' bench, seeing Mr. Geers blowing Napoleon Direct out or training My Rosebud, The Abbot, Direct Hal, or St. Frisco? And one can picture Fred Edman driving game Peter L. or William Dickerson driving Hollyrood Colin from the head of the stretch to win as he did at Lexington. And can't one fancy, too, that Freeport's "wizard of the sulky," M. E. McHenry, is driving Sonoma Girl or Locust Jack?

Of course, it is only a dream, but who, if he is honest, doesn't dream? For some of these days we will make our last trip to the winners' circle, there to join the friends who have gone before us and to await those still to come.

The old-time bookmaker laughingly used to say to a customer who wanted to bet on a horse that the book-maker thought didn't have a chance, "Just write your own ticket." Well, if I am allowed to write my own ticket I will choose the pacing mare, Zombrewer, 2:04¼, the dam of Peter the Brewer, who did so much for Nat Ray, and who was the grandam of the Greatest Grey, our world's champion trotter Greyhound, and go sailing into eternity astride her.

And maybe when I reach that spirit world I can slip away sometimes and find horses that gave me pleasure and success over the years, and give them friendly pats and caresses. Wouldn't it be wonderful to be again with poor little misunderstood La Paloma, or to gaze fondly at Twinkling Belle or Ora Main or Linnworthy or Rose Marie Abbe or Louis Direct, Leila Patchen, and a host of others? Some of these horses played important roles in the lives of other trainers, too. They may enjoy them also, for in the spirit world we shall be free of earth's plague of jealousy!